Publisher's Acknowledgements
Special thanks are due to the
Marian Goodman Gallery, New
York, and the **Lisson Gallery**,
London. We would also like to
thank the following authors
and publishers for their kind
permission to reprint articles:
Lynne Cooke, New York; **Editions
du Regard**, Paris; **Chapter Arts
Centre**, Cardiff; **The South Bank
Centre**, London; **Carnegie
Museum of Art**, Pittsburgh,
and the following for lending
reproductions: **Artangel**, London;
Camden Arts Centre, London;
Chisenhale Gallery, London;
Galerie Durand-Dessert, Paris;
Konrad Fischer Galerie,
Düsseldorf; **Jochen Gerz** and
Esther Shalev-Gerz, Germany;
Antony Gormley, London;
Government Art Collection,
London; **Musée d'art moderne de
Ceret**; **Open-Air Museum of
Sculpture Middelheim**, Antwerp;
Thomas Schütte, Düsseldorf; **Tate
Gallery**, London ; **Nina Williams
née Gabo**, Kent; and **Whitechapel
Art Gallery**, London.
Photographers: **Kristien Daem,
Dorothee Fischer, Frans
Grummer, Ralph Hinterkeuser,
Lisa Harty, Jorge Lewinski,
Attilio Maranzano, Pierre
Mercier, Helge Mundt, Sue
Ormerod, Tore Royneland, Ianthe
Ruthven, Adam Rzepka, Etienne
van Sloun, Stephen White,
Gareth Winters** and **Edward
Woodman**.

Artist's Acknowledgements
I would personally like to thank
Iwona Blazwick for her invitation
to do this book and to thank Clare
Stent, Gilda Williams, Stuart Smith
and everyone else involved at
Phaidon for their hard work on the
production of something so clear
from the murky depths of my
archives. I would also like to thank
Marian Goodman and Nicholas
Logsdail as well as Elizabeth
McCrae and Maria Prodromou at
the Lisson Gallery for all their help
and support, especially in the
gathering and sorting of
photographs and documentation.
It's a privilege to have Pier Luigi
Tazzi, Jon Thompson and Peter
Schjeldahl be engaged with one's
work and I thank them deeply for
their texts. Many photographers
have produced the images we have
used in this book, I want to thank
all of them for their time and
attention. I should like to record
my debt to Mathew Perry, with
whom I have worked for more than
ten years and whose contribution
has been immense. Similarly,
Derek Eversden took me seriously
when I asked his company to make
the steelwork for *Blind, Deaf and
Dumb* and thus began an
association which has borne many
fruit. These two I can never thank
enough.

All works are in private collections
unless otherwise stated.

Phaidon Press Limited
Regent's Wharf
All Saints Street
London N1 9PA

First published 1995
© Phaidon Press Limited 1995
All works of Richard Deacon are
© Richard Deacon.

ISBN 0 7148 33703

A CIP catalogue record of this book
is available from the British
Library.

Printed in Hong Kong

cover, **More Light**
1987-88
Aluminium, plywood
290 x 335 x 201 cm
Collection, St. Louis Art Museum,
Missouri

page 4, **Bikini**
1992
Aluminium, wood, epoxy resin
165 x 1200 x 350 cm
Installation, Documenta IX,
Kassel

page 6, **Stuff Box Object**
1970-71
Performance work

page 36, **Kiss and Tell** (detail)
1989
Epoxy, plywood, steel, timber
176 x 226 x 170 cm
Collection, Arts Council of Great
Britain, London

page 88, **Keeping the Faith**
(detail)
1992
Beechwood, epoxy
75 x 175 x 170 cm

page 98, **Artist's studio shelf**

page 144, **Richard Deacon and
Bill Woodrow**
Invitation card, 'Only the Lonely',
Chisenhale Gallery, London
1993

page 160, Drawing for **The Back of
My Hand No 1**
1986
Pencil and ink on paper
40 x 30 cm

Jon Thompson Pier Luigi Tazzi Peter Schjeldahl

Richard Deacon

Φ

Contents

Interview Pier Luigi Tazzi in conversation with **Richard Deacon, page 6.** **Survey** Jon Thompson Thinking Richard Deacon, Thinking Sculptor, Thinking Sculpture, **page 36.** **Focus** Peter Schjeldahl Deacon's Faith, **page 88.** **Artist's Choice** Mary Douglas Purity and Danger, 1966, **page 98.** **Artist's Writings** Richard Deacon Selections from Stuff Box Object, 1971-72, **page 110.** Artist's Statement, 1982, **page 114.** Silence, Exile, Cunning, 1986-88, **page 116.** What Car? Correspondence with Lynne Cooke, 1992 **page 120.** What You See Is What You Get, 1992, **page 132.** Design for *Replacing*, 1987, **page 138.** Design for *Factory*, 1993, **page 139.** Reading: a propos de Toni Grand, 1993, **page 140.** **Chronology** page 144 & Bibliography, **page 158.**

Contents

Interview **Pier Luigi Tazzi** in conversation with **Richard Deacon, page 6.** Survey Jon Thompson

Thinking Richard Deacon, Thinking Sculptor, Thinking Sculpture, **page 36.** Focus Peter Schjeldahl Deacon's Faith,

page 88. Artist's Choice Mary Douglas Purity and Danger, 1966, page 98. Artist's

Writings Richard Deacon Selections from Stuff Box Object, 1971-72, **page 110.** Artist's Statement, 1982, **page 114.**

Silence, Exile, Cunning, 1986-88, **page 116.** What Car? Correspondence with Lynne Cooke, 1992 **page 120.** What You See Is What

You Get, 1992, **page 132.** Design for *Replacing*, 1987, **page 138.** Design for *Factory*, 1993, **page 139.** Reading: a propos de Toni

Grand, 1993, **page 140.** Chronology page 144 & Bibliography, **page 158.**

Pier Luigi Tazzi I would like to start from the distant past. I have always felt that since the beginning of the modern, there was no place for art. Art was mostly an image in the mind, or a precious object. While it was still in the artist's studio it was as yet unborn, and when it was in a private or museum collection, it was the relic of a practice that took place elsewhere, a sort of unknown non-site that was ideologically akin to the concept of utopia. The work of art began to acquire its own space toward the late 1950s-early 1960s and this ultimately resulted in the gallery space. This was a real space which was increasingly defined over the course of the decade and which in a way contrasted with the museum, which was more abstract, separate from the reality of the outside world. Until at least the end of the 1960s the museum was the principal space for art and where art obtained its status. During that time we had a shift from the closed, sanctified museum space to the living, 'real' space of the gallery.

At the end of the 1960s-early 1970s, what first emerged in theoretical discourse was the term 'context', particularly in conceptual art. This term was increasingly defined and analyzed in its specificity; that is, art does not acquire its meaning in and of itself but in relation to the context in which it is set and brought into action.

When the gallery space came to lose its primacy and at the same time its effectiveness, the term 'context' emerged again but in a different way. Context is no longer intended as it had been in the discourse of conceptual art, but now points to a dissolved area where the work of art is placed although it does not define the context by virtue of its presence. At the same time, there is a demand today for context, a need for context. What I want to ask you then is, when did you start to take the context into consideration not only in the production of the work but in its very constitution? What do you mean by context?

Richard Deacon **At the start of the 70s, when I was a student, I was confused about the category of things I wanted to make. I wanted to make something and that involved the manipulation of materials, but the models that were on offer seemed to involve making plans and carrying them out. I felt that this was the wrong procedure. It was also a time when there was a lot of interest in time-based work and performance, so I combined the two interests and started making performance based work which involved the manipulation of materials over a given period of time. The notion that how you do something had relevance to the thing that you do was a very early part of my work. I used photographs to document it but I became much more interested in description as a means of documentation. It had time in it in a more interesting way than a photograph. At some point in the middle of the decade I abandoned using a performance base with all its connotations of documentation and reproduction, though there are certain elements which carry through from that. These works often extended over a period of time and involved the creation of materials. I found the vehicle cumbersome and thought that it was possible to condense those concerns into a single object. Somehow I changed the way I looked at what I was doing and began to think of my previous work as a training in how to make objects, learning how to avoid making plans. Also in the context of making performance I found myself uncomfortable with my personal presence. I felt that I didn't need to be there. That describes how I think about sculpture, about making my work ever since. Somehow that 'I don't need to be here' is a good way of describing**

the kind of autonomy that I think the work should have.

Tazzi What startled you most about your physical presence?

Deacon **At the time, I thought that the reason I was there was as an agency to enable the work to be made. I wanted a certain kind of equality between myself as an agency and the material as an actor; I thought that my uncertainties, my doubts and my decision making, that somehow 'me' was the performer in a kind of autobiographical sense which I found uncomfortable. I suppose the honest answer would be that performing that way seemed to say things that I wasn't planning to say. It made the work personal in a private rather than possibly expressive sense. Another possible reason was that I didn't need the audience. I was perfectly happy in a performance situation entirely by myself. If you don't need the audience then you don't need the documentation, so what you have at the end is what you intend to make, that's the full logic of it. I was quite happy with that for a while and then, ten years later, I decided that the sculpture I was making and the gallery which was its location were problematic. Your description of the work being unborn in the studio and already dead when it arrived at the collection was very good. The gallery developed this in between status of 'this is when the work lives'. If that's the case then in some sense the gallery determines the work. The museum legitimizes it and the gallery enables it, or causes it to be. Obviously a lot of the conceptual artists' position was precisely to do with articulating the ways in which the gallery does that. To follow the argument through removes any need to do anything at all, because the gallery causes and the museum justifies.**

Tazzi This is strange, you stopped performing because at a certain point you recognized that you didn't need an audience. But what the gallery space was offering was a stage without an audience, where the audience was not necessary because the stage in itself, the gallery space, was the place.

Deacon **Yes.**

Tazzi So in the gallery space you don't need an audience.

Deacon **It's implicit.**

Tazzi Yes it's implicit, it's already there. The stage, the sacred place is there. I think that your decision, and that of many other artists, was to confirm the primacy of the gallery space.

Deacon **At some point later I began to wonder whether it was a necessary truth and whether the context was not necessarily defined by the gallery; in fact you could turn it upside down and have the making or the thing that was made define the context. So the gallery was a part but not necessarily the whole. I have often talked about works that I have made on three scales: small, medium size and large works. The small works are domestic, the medium works are gallery size and the large works are public. But there is a continuity between all of them and therefore if you look at context you would look for something that overarched all those three scales. At some**

point I wanted to make things that didn't fit inside the gallery. I thought there might be other contexts for the work, other places to put things where they could still function as art objects. Obviously there are lots of places where they probably don't function as art objects. I made some things which were placed out in the park. I found that didn't work, it was just taking one thing and putting it somewhere else, which seemed an inadequate solution. In 1985 I did this show at the Serpentine Gallery with the work *Blind, Deaf and Dumb*, which used a link through the wall of the gallery to a work that was outside. I used the window and the building as a means, and tried to make the architecture be contained by the work, rather than be a container.

Tazzi That also occurred with your contribution to the 1985 Biennale of Paris. It had the same aim in a way. The three works, *Other Homes Other Lives, Like a Bird* and *Tell Me No Lies*, were in overt contradiction with the architectural space of the Grande Halle de la Villette. There was a sort of fight between the architecture and your works. The architecture was not the container of the work: there was a sort of dialogue with the architecture itself. Most of the other works in that show were simply contained in a building which falls into the category of industrial archaeology. In your case the contrast was extremely evident.

Deacon **The exhibition in Paris was precisely between having made works which had been placed outside, and my being unsatisfied with that, and doing the work in the Serpentine, where I was more aggressive towards the architecture. Those were intuitive decisions. I removed myself to the outside in Paris, to the exterior of the building; I didn't want to be within the big hall. A part of it was in order to establish a relationship between the work and the building that had some purpose to it, that wasn't temporary.**

Blind, Deaf and Dumb A
1985
Laminated wood, glue
873.7 × 99 × 312.4 cm
Installation, Serpentine Gallery,
London
Collection, Rijksmuseum Kröller
Müller, Otterlo

following pages, **Blind, Deaf and Dumb B**
1985
Galvanized steel
370.8 × 800 × 381 cm
Installation outside Serpentine
Gallery, London

Blind, Deaf and Dumb
Preproduction drawing
1985
Pencil on paper
41 × 56 cm

Blind, Deaf and Dumb
Preproduction drawing
1985
Pencil on paper
41 × 56 cm

Tazzi In fact one of the feelings I had – it's rather banal, maybe a little simplistic but it might explain something – was that one never knew whether your sculpture came before the building or the building came before your sculpture. There was an overlapping, but at the same time there was no fusion between the building, your sculpture, and the overlapping itself. Also, you were going against one of the most substantial characteristics of architecture: the possibility of opening and closing space at its own discretion. With your work, this possibility is denied. In other words, architecture implies that a given space can be closed. It is not a question of establishing a flexible articulation between aperture and enclosure. The fundamental fact is that enclosure is in any case a possibility. Think of the cave, the first building constructed by humankind, the defence systems brought forth during the Renaissance – all things from which modern architecture is derived. I thought your sculptures were like bars in the door, keeping the door open.

Deacon **Well, that's what they should be. Because I was really unhappy about being given a cubicle in a big space, it was very much a 'fuck you, I don't want to do this, I'd much rather be outside'. What I was starting to say earlier was that autonomy becomes a more important term the longer it goes on. The procedures I had for making work tend to involve a certain kind of wrapping up of space. They became sort of circular motions. The autonomy has to do with that decision, that you don't need the audience, you think that somehow the object should be completely contained, wrapped up in itself.**

Tazzi Thinking about that show in connection with what we are talking about now, I remember other works that had a completely different relationship not only with the architecture, but with the physical, formal and historical context. Particularly Luciano Fabro's work, which was outside trying to haul the whole building in a sort of metaphor of history. Or the work of Ulrich Rückriem, which was completely detached from the building, like a timeless mark of the presence of art or of human action.

Ulrich Rückriem
Untitled
1985
Installation, Biennale de Paris

Deacon The reason I started making performance work at the end of the 60s was because I wanted to make, but I didn't know what. I suppose in a way it is still a problem. There is a kind of fixity to Rückriem's work that creates a problematic for me. This isn't a critique of the work; indeed there is a relationship. I wanted to make work that didn't involve gravity in the classical way that Rückriem's work belongs to gravity, with his simple operations on the block. The work is always subject to gravity and place in a very definite way. Material and its manipulation are core areas in what I do. Matter, stuff, are the words I tend to use. Matter is a ground for the work in relation to its existence rather than its weight, or its mass. Weight was always a difficult thing for me. My idea about sculpture was that it was composed of matter but wasn't subject to gravity. This is metaphorical, obviously, but I thought of sculpture as being between me and the world, rather than sitting in the world.

Tazzi In other terms – not artistic terms – the works of Rückriem have to do with erection. It is a phallic work in any case, where the phallus is important as a sign in its symbolic function as an archaeological point of reference and orientation. Rückriem reflects quite closely Jacques Lacan's reading of Sigmund Freud in which the phallus is not a phantom in the sense of being a figure. Nor is it an object, nor the organ itself. It is a simulacrum, a signifier whose prime meaning is 'to be or not to be', to be there, to be erect with a specific mass, a specific material, worked in a specific – and simple – way. On the other hand you consider the substance of the phallus independently of its function as a signifier, or its erection and its erectibility.

Deacon Yes I suppose so. I could put it another way; Rückriem's work is clearly made of material, and the material sits in the world. For me, material, matter, is much closer to being human, is much less alienated from being human than that opposition of the physical object grounded in the world. Matter is much closer to language and I wanted to make sculpture that showed that aspect of belonging to the human more than belonging to the world. When we speak to each other we use something that is common, that doesn't really belong to any of us. We can extract meaning from it and use it to signify, but what enables us to do that is its commonalty, we all agree on it. I wanted to make sculpture that was being more like that than it was to being fixed. The area I was trying to explore has to do with allowing material to have form and at the same time to be able to be formed. There is a certain indefiniteness or ambiguity to a lot of the things that I do in relationship to what they might look like, and at the same time the great specificity of material and of the substance of the work is clear. The form is clear but there's also a desire for a potential plasticity or fluidity which remains latent. In a sense I have been trying to attach sculpture to perception or to experience rather than attaching it to the world. A contemporary analogy is to talk of a

Installation, Biennale de Paris
1985
l. to r., **Like a Bird**, 1984; **Other Homes, Other Lives**, 1984-85; **Tell Me No Lies**, 1984

virus and the way a virus attacks the host. **The problematic is to try and make sculpture that is parasitic upon the perception of the host rather than sculpture that is in and of the world.**

Tazzi Yes, but when I use the term 'timeless' for the work of Rückriem, I meant just that, to be not against culture but before culture, to go back to a certain archetype, to go back to a certain source. Your work is far more linked to the evolution of language; Rückriem's language is very elementary, whereas your language is much more articulated. What Rückriem is doing is establishing the scan of the language, the primal gap.

Deacon Yes, possibly. Clearly I don't make work that's primal.

Tazzi What I find in common between your works and Rückriem's are at least two things. You share what you called autonomy, and this common base, common ground, even if the articulation is completely different.

Deacon You mean a material base, a material ground.

Tazzi Yes, that was quite important in the early 70s, that had been achieved.

Deacon Well, it was something that was achieved, and also something that was made available. It was clearly a gain, or an opportunity. If you look at Donald Judd and Anthony Caro as two artists of very similar age, I think surprisingly for such an apparently restricted artist as Judd, the opening he and others made at the time is very clear. The way I put it, Judd doesn't tell you what to do, but he leaves a lot of things to do it with, whereas Caro tells you what to do. The heritage of Caro is stylistic whereas the heritage of Judd is fundamental.

Tazzi Caro and even more so Donald Judd have already become part of history, they have already been absorbed in contemporary art, whereas Rückriem remains as yet not digested.

Deacon Yes, I agree. It's surprising, a good quality. After the Serpentine in '85 there was the show in the park at Sonsbeek in '86 and through the city of Münster in '87. The curator of Sonsbeek, Saskia Bos, had a fairly complex idea about a glass house and a floating pavilion. Partly I suppose that her reason for proposing the pavilions was to underline an aspect of contemporary art practice which was denatured and artificial because of the history of the space as an artificial park. For me it coincided with doing a lot of reading about the picturesque in the eighteenth century and the ways in which the world was seen as expressive and signifying. I was also interested at the time in geological history, very ancient history and the intellectual processes in relationship to the investigation of the earth as an ancient geological item. There was a way in which intellectual operations could picture a world different to the world we inhabit, although it's the same place. In the eighteenth century nature disappeared and was replaced by construction, by a human-centred world.

Tazzi The relationship between city and country was completely reversed.

Installation, Fruitmarket Gallery, Edinburgh
1984
l. to r., **Two Can Play**, 1983; **Like a Bird**, 1984; **Untitled**, 1980; **For Those Who Have Ears No. 2**, 1983; **On the Face of It**, 1984; **Tall Tree in the Ear**, 1983-84

Donald Judd
Installation, Whitechapel Art Gallery, London
1973

Deacon **And the park at Sonsbeek is a representation. My work was a rigid frame, with an undefined element within it but situated in a place, between the war memorial and the villa. In some sense the physical object and the manifestations of ideology within the various elements of the park – its construction, its buildings, the war memorial, etc. – were all pictures, constructions. What I was trying to make the work do was to be equivalent to the park and to the spectator, so there were three elements: the work, the park and the spectator. They were more or less in balance.**

Tazzi I found your work at Sonsbeek, *When the Land Masses First Appeared*, extraordinary. It was one of the emblematic works of the exhibition for the relation between the container, the rigid form outside, and the contained shape, the organic free form inside. This relationship was very opposite to the notion of the park, where the natural is the outside world and the design of the park is the inside world. This relationship, in connection to what we were saying before about context, revealed the distance taken from the idea of context as it had been defined by conceptual art. For the first time I could experience through that work something I had not understood before. The context had not been defined by known components and certain elements resisted all definition and categorization and remained unstable. The context had to do with an essence of which you had no knowledge: a sort of first step into outer space, with all its contingent risks. It had the freshness and happiness of a first discovery, like a baby's first word, or like some works from the Italian Renaissance, or in some Impressionist paintings. They have the same kind of dawn, when the day is approaching and everything is pale and bright; the colours are extremely distinct, not attacking your perception, but arriving with the renewal of your perception after a night's sleep and with the morning light. Saskia Bos' project was to create this primeval garden, a kind of Eden. Your work in Münster, *Like a Snail*, was again contextualized in a bureaucratic way, the work of art in relation to the urban context and vice versa. The two were well-differentiated, despite the resulting revelation that the chaos of the urban context opposed the positive affirmation of the work of art. This distinction appeared so evidently there for the first time. But the context, likewise, was no longer open but closed in its definition as an urban landscape. Your work stood in relation to architecture as a complement to an established environment.

Deacon **That's correct.**

Tazzi My reference to the light of dawn was not merely a poetic digression, it was in reference to the title of an early work of Anthony Caro's, *Early One Morning*. This seems a characteristic of British art when it reaches a turning point.

Deacon **Yes, I know that work. To digress a bit, one of the differences was that I knew what I was doing in Münster but I didn't know what I was doing in Sonsbeek. One of the problems for me as an artist and maybe for artists in general is to be in situations where you don't know what you are doing in a productive way. You can't always do that. I think you are correct to say that the intention was articulated and the context was clearly established. To be brief about it, I said 'I want to make a work that is the equivalent of a house'. In practical terms, *Blind, Deaf and Dumb* at the Serpentine Gallery, *When the Land Masses First Appeared* at Sonsbeek, and *Like a Snail* at Münster qualified me in terms of experience to think about and to be offered opportunities to make work in other places. One was in Krefeld, another was in Los Angeles, and there were some commissions that resulted. The work in Krefeld is one of the longest, begun in '88 and finished in '92. Do you know this work?**

Tazzi Yes.

Deacon **I didn't really know what to call it. Sometimes it's quite easy for me to title works, in this case the work is titled in relationship to intention.**

above, **When the Land Masses First Appeared**
1986
Laminated wood, zinc-sprayed steel
225 × 650 × 750 cm
Installation, Sonsbeek '86, Arnhem

left, **Anthony Caro**
Early One Morning
1962
Painted metal
290 × 620 × 335 cm

following pages
left, **Like a Snail A**
1987
Steel, hardboard, timber, plywood
500 × 650 × 450 cm
Installation, Münster Sculpture Project
Collection, Tochigi Prefectural Museum, Japan

right, **This Is Not a Story**
1992
Stainless steel
400 × 500 × 300 cm
Waiblingen, Germany

above, **Like a Snail B**

1987

Laminated wood, aluminium

$600 \times 500 \times 500$ cm

Installation, Münster Sculpture
Project

Sometimes work is titled in relationship to image. The work is called *Building from the Inside*. The place that I found and wanted to use in Krefeld was one of those urban spaces which mean nothing, a kind of open space without any real function, where roads met, that happened to define an area of ground. There are various ways you can think about the work as an entrance. I think you are correct to point out that *Like a Snail* in Münster was in relationship to a defined context, the elements were clear. In Krefeld it's a more risky operation because the context is undefined. The attempt was really to make a work which defines the context rather than opposing or establishing it. The place has negative qualities; it's not really the city or the country. There are various rebuilding plans for the area. The meaning of the work comes from the inside; its attempt is to generate the place, rather than the other way round, with the place generating the work. There are lots of dimensions to that: political, social, cultural, the idea about public.

Tazzi Can *Building from the Inside* in Krefeld be distinguished from what is called public art? You cannot consider the Münster piece public art, it was a component of the overall project, but in Krefeld there were links.

Deacon It's not the only one; there are other works in public places. I have some problems with the term public art; the other term is art in public spaces, and there is obviously a discourse around that. The problem I have with the term public art is that it implies a degree of social engineering, that it is something that is good for you, like medicine or public housing. But at the same time it has a certain freedom, a free availability, the public domain. When I was making *Building from the Inside* for Krefeld I was doing a number of other projects and talking to various people. It was a time in the late 80s when a confusion between the private and the public space came into being, public space got privatized, particularly in Britain. The plaza became an extension of the commercial space rather than a freely available place. It was characterized for me in the late 80s by a car advertisement which seemed to place a car in that public position. Ideologically I began to wonder whether the sense of openness implied in the notion of the public space was a component in the experience of art, and that in some ways sculpture is in the public domain. The work in Krefeld was an attempt to make an opening in space of a particular sort, to create a potential, and to act as a generator for the space that surrounds it. It's not a sign, it's not a logo, it's not a monument. I've tried to use the interiority of architecture as an element, as an appropriated mode. In Krefeld you could say that I was trying to appropriate publicness to the work, and to put that into the experience of what one has as the spectator. One of the limits of autonomy might not be architecture but publicness. There might be a point in which the social context inhibits or provides a limit to the work. I have wanted to make the connection of the plasticity of material to humanness a feature of the work. Therefore in some senses the human and human experience become a determining context. Another way to put it would be to say that if the work implies that it might belong to the social context then that's OK; if it belongs to the social context then it becomes something else. There might well be a point when the work ceases to be sculpture and becomes architecture. What's interesting is the edge between the two, the extent from which you borrow from one in order to enrich or enlarge the experience of the other.

Building from the Inside
1992
Stainless steel
613 × 745 × 370 cm
Voltaplatz, Krefeld, Germany

Nobody Here But Us
1991
Painted aluminium
555 × 505 × 945 cm
Installed, A. J. B. Bank Centre,
Auckland, New Zealand

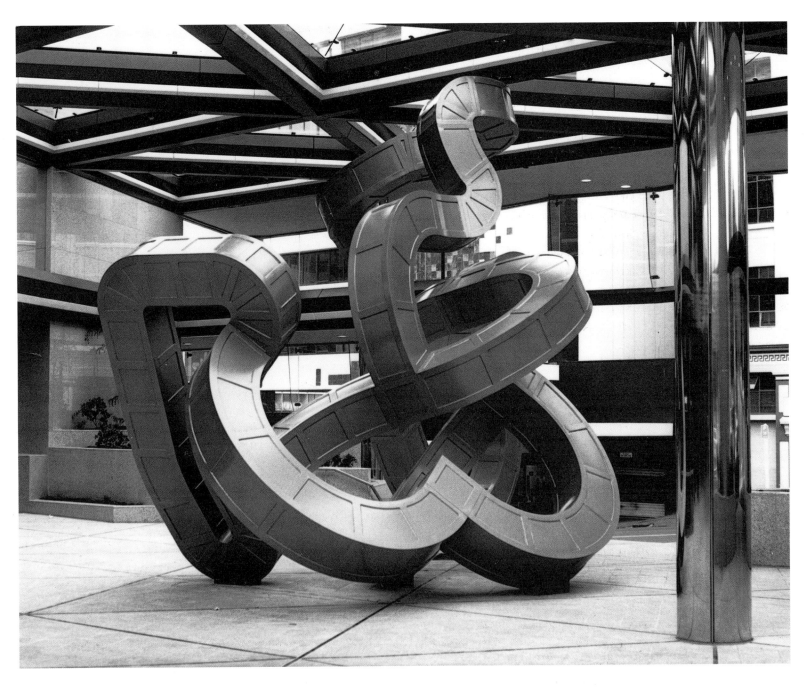

Tazzi There is also another difference between Münster and Krefeld. The context in Münster was connotated by signs and signifiers, whereas in Krefeld the relationship of your work was more with being in an undefined place than with the users of these signs and signifiers.

Deacon **In Münster the context was also established by the fact that this was a temporary exhibition. When you see this or that thing within the city you think, 'oh this is part of the Münster exhibition'. That's the first experience, before you explore the particularities of the work. In Krefeld what makes it particularly interesting is the relationship to other things, to plants, trees, houses, people. So the question of 'what is this', the immediate relationship, is not to an exhibition but to other elements and to other things within the work and to the spectator's own expectations, experiences, history and so on.**

Tazzi In Münster it is a sign alongside other signs. Of course *Like a Snail* in

Pipe
1991
Aluminium
142 × 437 × 175 cm
Installation outside Haus Lange,
Krefeld

Münster has a different quality than the other urban signs and this difference is marked by an opposition. In Krefeld the opposition is not so relevant; there is no real opposition, there is a sort of coexistence. In terms of the relationship of art and architecture, your exhibition inside Haus Esters and Haus Lange proposed another series of problems. In that case the relationship was between two disciplines – your work and historically established architecture recognized as being of good quality. It looked more like a laboratory experiment, something done in vitro.

**The Interior Is Always More
Difficult (C, E, F)**
1991
Paint and vinyl on plastic sheet
with aluminium frames
C, 233 × 361.5 cm
E, 234 × 348.5 cm
F, 233.5 × 272.5 cm
Installation, Haus Lange, Krefeld

Deacon I think showing what you do is implicit in the act of making art, and there are models for doing it. The exhibition is currently one of the strongest models around. For artists, to make an exhibition is to a greater or lesser extent a continuation of what happens in the studio. Showing what you do is one of the first consequences or elements of the practice. So the basic model is that you make one thing and you show it to someone else. There are expectations on both sides, and that generates the context and has physical as well as ideological dimensions. The relationship between things is a component in how you understand the particular thing, which is what makes group exhibitions somehow more difficult than individual exhibitions, or more interesting. Haus Esters and Haus Lange are two similar buildings both by Mies van der Rohe next door to each other, but they are separate, and to get from one to the other you have to go outside and then inside. One model would be to assume that the transition from one space to the other is mechanical and there is continuity between the two places, that you are just walking down the corridor. I thought the fact that there were two spaces made it possible to use two models of showing. In Haus Esters the model was conventional as it was understood in late 80s art practice: the work was individually autonomous and contained in the rooms. The scale of the work suggested pressing against the container, but nevertheless it was contained. There was a single work which was repeated in the other house to provide a link between the two spaces, and in the Haus Lange the simplest thing to say would be that I wanted to turn it inside out. There was a work outside the front door and work out the back and on the windows. The major work inside was transparent. At the same time the individual autonomy of the works was respected. The intention in Haus Lange was always to put the viewer in the wrong place in relationship to the work, so that it was either in their way or they were unable to get to it. There was no ideal position for the spectator in relationship to the work, whereas in Haus Esters the spectator was correctly located and physically present in relationship to the work. In Haus Lange the suggestion was that you would experience a desire to be somewhere else in order to gain the correct view, or in order to understand. That displacement wasn't intended aggressively, it was an inversion in order to shake the model. There is another model which is broadly constructed around the notion of installation where the physical, social or spatial context has a very strong determining influence on the work but disappears outside of the installation. But I did want to press this exhibition model, in part in order to emphasize autonomy and physical continuity within the spectator's view of the work and to make the building less solid.

Tazzi This was quite clear, but all that implied a sort of dialogue with the absoluteness and the ideology of form, expressed by the architecture of Mies van der Rohe. It implied a new reading of history, a relationship with history, with something already there and of historical value. A living artist has to deal with that through his work. In this sense, again the relationship is with the 'other', with the unknown.

Deacon **The two houses are canonical spaces; their dimensions are as much in the realm of idea and history as they are physical. I'd like it if they weren't appropriated by history, that they continued to vibrate. One of the problems of showing there is that you can celebrate it, ignore it or try and do something else; I was trying to do something which didn't demean the architecture but wasn't awestruck in relation to it. It was ambitious and egotistical in that I wanted to be on the same level as the architecture. In a way the architecture takes you to the garden. The big windows are intended to idealize the garden. The house is almost closed to the street.**

Tazzi And the windows always frame the garden outside.

Deacon **By blocking off the windows with screens, a shape was imposed between the house and the garden. From the house you'd see it as in the garden; from the garden you'd see it as in the house. Intellectually I was trying to put something in the way which had to be put aside to be able to see the house. Basically it was an irritant intended to bring forward the house as well as the work.**

Tazzi There was an opposition: you decided to interrupt the transparency which was one of the principal characteristics in Mies van der Rohe's project.

Deacon **The transparency of the big work made of plastic, *Pack*, was 'removed' from the house.**

Tazzi The material was, like other works of yours, very evident. Not only the forms were relevant but the material too, especially because of its translucence.

Deacon **I'm quite clumsy; things aren't as pristine as I tend to think of them; I am less capable than I think, but the work gets less interesting when I get too clean. I think it's a quality in my work that has some value, that the material has a sense of the specific to it.**

Tazzi What was relevant wasn't the transparent quality of the material but the material itself.

Deacon **Yes, it was congealed.**

Tazzi If the reason to use that material on the work inside was because of its transparent quality, the result was a kind of presence. Again, not the function but the substance.

Deacon **Yes, I agree with that. But substance seems more interesting to me than function, it has more depth. The transparency of the plastic work gets converted to a sense of materiality and substance rather than function. Despite the work being transparent it has a physical appearance.**

Henry Moore
Recumbent Figure
1938
Hornton stone
l. 134 cm

Antony Gormley
Three Ways: Mould, Hole and
Passage
1981
Lead, fibreglass, plaster
Mould, 60 × 98 × 50 cm
Hole, 62 × 123 × 80 cm
Passage, 34 × 209 × 50 cm

Installation, Haus Lange, Krefeld
l. to r., **Pack**
1990
Welded PVC
217 × 253 × 159 cm
Border
1991
Wood, welded PVC
48 × 335 × 171 cm

Untitled
1991
Beaten copper
122 × 205 × 91 cm
Installation, Haus Esters, Krefeld
Collection, Krefelder
Kunstmuseum

Tazzi Also important to me, considering the peculiarities of the buildings, was that there are no references to the fact that in many of Mies van der Rohe's drawings there are explicit suggestions as to what kind of art – painting and sculpture – his architecture is meant to host. And among the ideal works for his spaces are the sculptures of Henry Moore, which appear quite often. Henry Moore's works are far more dependent on architecture than one would expect. In the ideology of form as confirmed by Mies van der Rohe, the work of art was included as a sort of spiritual element within the rational structure of the architecture. Architecture as a container of spirituality, spirituality represented by the work of art. And Henry Moore followed this guideline.

Deacon **I suppose so.**

Tazzi I have been considering this relationship between Mies van der Rohe and Henry Moore, because in your work you are refusing this concept.

Deacon **Part of the problem with that has to do with spirituality, doesn't it?**

Tazzi It has to do with formalization. In a way a work of Henry Moore needs a frame; even if it's sculpture, it needs a frame. What Mies van der Rohe is generally doing through all his work is to build a frame.

Deacon **Well, in the best buildings there is an extraordinary fluidity of space and ambiguity between interior and exterior, particularly true of the German pavilion in Barcelona. Another way is to say that within that fluidity Henry Moore served a purpose of being solid, like lumps … icebergs in the sea. There are points of concretization within the flow.**

Tazzi In a way the solidity that Mies van der Rohe was searching for had the same character, the same solidity as African sculpture in the eyes of Picasso.

Deacon **Do you mean it was real?**

Tazzi Yes, and they shared the same kind of approach, solidity and spirituality in the same object at the same time.

Deacon **I accept that. The solidity was also in respect of human presence, so they are not humanless lumps. Lumps is a parody; there is some sense that the flux, the flow within the frame is one element, and against that you have something static. Both the frame and the lump are humanly determined.**

Tazzi In your work the solidity is far more a sort of encumbrance that doesn't allow one to go with the space, which blocks the way.

Deacon **Yes, that's what I mean. The body in my work is used as an encumbrance or obstruction, used as flesh and not used as a sign of transcendence or idealization. Antony Gormley uses the body as a metaphor for the transcendent subject, but at the same time the body is that in which you live. One of the ways in which I intend you to experience my work is as if you are in front of another person and in terms of a relationship to particular bodily sensations. When I began making** sculptures the procedures that I used were intended to make the act of work create the form and input structure into the material. Structure and material and form were all equally present on the surface; there was no hierarchy between those elements. At the same time the centre was left independent of those elements, so in that sense the ambiguity in the work had to do with the specificities of appearance. I tend to incorporate all those things in relationship to an empty interior.

Tazzi The exhibitions we've discussed thus far all implied a relationship with a context, even if the notion of context has changed and has been modified by the evolution of the work of artists, not only personal evolution but in changing ways of presenting art. How is the relationship with context expressed in some exhibitions, like the one in Oslo, or, more recently, in Hanover? At first glance they looked – especially the one in Oslo – like canonical gallery shows. And you've told me that both of them have been quite important for you.

Heart and Mind
1986
Laminated hardboard, satin,
screws
185 × 230 × 45 cm

Deacon **I've made a lot of things where one work is made for one occasion. I've also done travelling exhibitions which I don't like because there is a balance between place and work which seems necessary to construct. In Hanover and Oslo the work was carefully selected to make a particular ensemble for an occasion. It's normal exhibition making – there is a possibility to cause, permit or prohibit. I make works in many different ways, but obviously there are repetitions, of material, of technique and of form. But individual works also have autonomy.**

Tazzi I don't want to be over-systematic but I feel there are two strains in your work. One goes from the exhibition in Paris and reaches the work in Middelheim, (*Never Mind*), in which there is a recognizable tension between the work and its surroundings. The other emerges through exhibitions like the one in Oslo or at Locus Solus in Genoa. In these it's not an integration but a sympathy with the place; place not only as an architectural feature but also in terms of the aura. The exhibitions at Locus Solus, *Bikini* at Documenta IX, or at Feuerle, where your sculptures were set alongside antique tea pots, all have something in common: the search for an equilibrium between the work of art and its surroundings as something which possesses a peculiar quality – in the same way that the works have a special value for you as the maker.

Deacon **The work on the bridge in Plymouth, *Moor*, would also be within this sympathetic relationship.**

Tazzi By sympathetic relationship I also mean a certain passive attitude, as opposed to an active one: it attempts to be receptive to the surroundings, to be open to the aura, not to signal difference and impose the mark of the artist or of his/her actions. Sympathy then is more as reception than an effort to mark difference, all the while maintaining the autonomy of the work in that particular environment.

Deacon **The question is, what is the relationship between the two modalities and …**

Moor
1990
Painted mild steel
500 × 2475 × 350 cm
Commissioned for TSWA Four Cities
Project
Victoria Park, Plymouth

Tazzi I don't know whether they should be conceived as two strains or two modalities or just a side effect on the part of the observer.

Deacon **If we accept this distinction then I suppose the experience of looking at art has modalities within it. If you take the line from the Paris shows through, there would seem to be a development in the work towards autonomy, to putting the spectator in the position of being equal but at the same time separate from the work, to separate the elements within a given experience: me, the works, the park etc. I think I do work in two ways. It seems to me an intriguing thing and an extraordinary possibility that under the umbrella of making autonomous objects there are aspects of one's experience in the world that are sometimes separated and sometimes coherent, and it is possible to make objects that characterize those two modalities. This is partly a discussion that is prefigured in the twentieth century with abstraction and empathy. There are works from the beginning of the 80s that attempt to do both things at once, works to which you have an empathetic response. I think that in the work I do there is a sense of**

connection between those two modalities. In a puritanical sense, for example, the work in Middelheim, *Never Mind*, has many qualities that I regard as highly desirable in a work of art. The way in which the work of art resists appropriation by the spectator or the place seem to me to be highly desirable features. I am less sure that the harmonious relationship of the work to the space is of the same value. I like Bernini's sculpture very much which surprises me because it has degrees of sensuousness which as a puritanical North European I find myself suspicious of, in relation to something like authenticity. If you enjoy it, it can't really be good. So I have to fight against that element within my character, because it's stupid as a reaction and has nothing to do with it. There is nothing wrong with beauty, and what I would really like to do would be to make work which would put those two things together. It may be impossible because you are trying to put dependence and independence into the same thing. But I would like to fuse those two things together.

Tazzi The big problem is the condition in which the work of art has to take place. So when I refer to a sympathetic relationship I see an attempt at protecting this modality. In the other modality I see exactly the contrary, the risk of encountering the unknown, the risk of losing control.

Deacon **I think you are right.**

Tazzi This takes us back to the beginning of the conversation, when we were discussing how the term context has changed. It used to be that context was some sort of structure which hosted a work of art, a conceptual device which established a link between the work of art and the world, which in turn was conceived of as a fixed structure. That structure has to protect and emphasize the value of the work of art in itself. Not the value in absolute terms but in itself; the validity, not the authenticity of the work of art. At the end of this *parcours* we find that the context is exactly the contrary: it doesn't protect the work of art but pushes it out of its traditional protection, into the risks of the world. Its systemic structure not only is no longer effective, but some of its components have yet to be defined and some are completely out of control. In a sense this is also the *parcours* through your work; things are always going from inside to outside and vice versa, meeting the void and encompassing it through a great many procedures, without being afraid and at the same time seeking the security of an established place. Ultimately, again it is the problem of what the place for art is now. Since this notion of context has completely changed over the past twenty years, what can the new structure be, the new possibility for coherent articulation, the new framework in which art can be placed? Where might art find its place?

Deacon **But surely the interesting thing is to keep the framework uncertain; if you make a new framework then you establish a new convention. What interests me is to retain an uncertainty within the framework, because then you are dealing with something you don't know. If the framework is determined then really you have the Academy. What's interesting about the disruptions in the context that we've been discussing seem to be as much negative as they are positive. In a sense the consequence of the fracture of the monolithic ideas about history is that modalities for perception have**

previous pages, Installation, Kunstnernes Hus, Oslo
1989
l. to r., **Tear**; **Seal**; **Mammoth**

following pages, **Never Mind**
1993
Wood, stainless steel, epoxy
310 × 765 × 300 cm
Middelheim Sculpture Park, Antwerp

alternatives. Authority is broken and values are relative rather than absolute. The very experience of the work of art has a degree of relativity. In some ways I am a very conventional artist and I produce a conventional object. I am attached to an idea about a tradition, but I think that that attachment isn't necessarily one way. It's a means, not a value. So when we were talking about the modalities earlier, to go from one to the other is possibly to say it's all bullshit, to make you feel comfortable with a situation. The problem with relativity is that it's a moving target and enables all things to be made equal and nothing to be determined. That's the stick I have to beat myself with. That question. But it's not necessary if one framework has gone to suggest an alternative, because there may be several alternatives. The difficulty is that if there are several alternatives, that lowers the possibilities in any of them; making judgements becomes more difficult, because there are alternative criteria. You can't make judgements from the same surety because there is always another possible position to take up.

Tazzi The problem is not that we are in the absence of context, but that the idea of context has changed. When this notion first came out the context was defined through analyses. The instruments had a certain credibility and were considered 'scientific'. They had this kind of aspiration to truth in a way, whereas in the current situation what is lacking is this kind of credibility. The instruments of generalization are no longer effective enough to provide an image of the status of things.

Deacon **Yes, but that's a product of relativization. And it seems to me inescapable.**

Tazzi Yes. If we are currently in a moment of mutation then it's time to be very careful about the kind of mutation going on. Not in terms of judgement but in terms of survival. If in 1968, for instance, everybody was talking about how to achieve a better quality of life, today the issue is different: it's life, it's survival. That's completely different.

Deacon **One of the dimensions in the political debate in this country at the moment has to do with morality. The sense expressed by Conservative politicians is that the consequence of 1968 has been the degeneration of public morality. And that this is a crisis of value, a crisis of democratic institutions, a crisis of society. The offered solution is regressive; yet at the same time the crisis is a consequence of the pursuit of values promoted by the same political ideology that now fears the situation which it has created. This has some overlap with what you were saying. In the domain of art practice you are left in the situation in which you have had both models taken away from you at the same time. The collapse of social values associated with the left and a collapse of the moral, individualistic values associated with the right. The resolution of the contradiction will be reliant on a reconstruction of the idea of society or not.**

Contents

Interview Pier Luigi Tazzi in conversation with Richard Deacon, page 6. Survey Jon Thompson

Thinking Richard Deacon, Thinking Sculptor, Thinking Sculpture, page 36. Focus Peter Schjeldahl Deacon's Faith,
page 88. Artist's Choice Mary Douglas Purity and Danger, 1966, page 98. Artist's
Writings Richard Deacon Selections from Stuff Box Object, 1971-72, page 110. Artist's Statement, 1982, page 114.

Silence, Exile, Cunning. 1986-88, page 116. What Car? Correspondence with Lynne Cooke, 1992 page 120. What You See Is What

You Get, 1992, page 132. Design for Replacing, 1987, page 138. Design for Factory, 1993, page 139. Reading: a propos de Toni

Grand, 1993, page 140. Chronology page 144 & Bibliography, page 158.

It's Orpheus When There's
Singing No 3
1978-79
Pencil on paper
112 × 147.5 cm

It's Orpheus When There's
Singing No 4
1978-79
Pencil on paper
112 × 147.5 cm

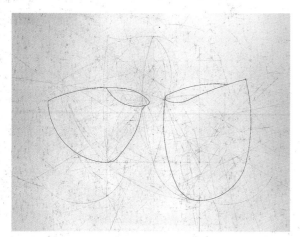

According to Homeric legend, it was Hermes, the messenger of the gods, who invented writing. And the story has it that he first of all confided his invention to Zeus, adding that he intended to make a gift of it to humankind. Zeus, apparently, was not enthusiastic and begged him not to do so, fearing that it would result in the loss of human memory.

For us today, this odd little story with its roots in the pre-textual world, can be seen as an expression of an exemplary fear: that through the all-pervasive power of coded inscription something important has been lost; a sense of connectedness or wholeness perhaps; the deep knowledge of social life which subsists in the community of bodies. The issue framed by this story then, is not simply about the human capacity to recall hard information, but more about writing's tendency to dismember and disperse the human subject. If we can be forgiven the impudence of attributing human thought to the mind of a god. Zeus, who we might take as being all-knowing, was surely never so naive as to have suggested that through the invention of writing, human beings would cease to be able to remember anything at all – the date of the battle of Hastings, family birthdays, or where they had parked the car – but that the regulated space of written language might render some of the shared aspects of human knowledge, immemorial.

This notion of a primal linguistic space – a domain of language which exists prior to the sign – in which the potential for human communication is neither distanced nor over-determined by the constraining rules of syntax, has continued to haunt modern linguistics. Roland Barthes, for example, in a key short article of 1975, *The Rustle*

of Language[1], writes about the possibility of such a space in almost euphoric terms, describing it as an 'expanded' even 'limitless' space, constituted out of the 'music of meaning'. In this 'utopic space', language he argues, 'would be enlarged to the point of forming a vast auditory fabric in which the semantic apparatus would be made unreal' and the 'phonic, metric signifier would be deployed in all its sumptuosity, without ever becoming detached from it … '. Here, meaning would persist without being 'brutally dismissed' or 'dogmatically foreclosed' by the functional imperatives of the sign. Indeed, to use Barthes' own words, 'it would be liberated from all the aggressiveness of which the sign, formed in the sad and fierce history of men, is the Pandora's Box'.

This dream of returning to a social space formed out of live communicative transactions finds an interesting echo in an early text by Richard Deacon, *Silence, Exile, Cunning*[2], a retrospective reflection on a series of drawings made during his stay in America in 1978/79. Deacon has described this particular year as a 'turning point'[3] in his development as an artist, and the drawings in question, collectively titled *It's Orpheus When There's Singing*, as providing something akin to 'a grammar': as standing in anticipation of the work that was to follow.

In America Deacon had read and re-read Rainer Maria Rilke's *Sonnets to Orpheus* and in the process found himself greatly attracted to the poet's lyric conceptualization of 'being' – grounded in musicality, vocalization and the mobility and independence of the body in dance. This seemed to offer an antidote to the formal stiffness (Deacon's

Out of His Own Mouth
1987-88
Plywood, vinyl, copper
132 × 175 × 83 cm
Collection, Museum of Modern
Art, New York

preceding pages, Installation,
Marian Goodman Gallery, New York
1986
l. to r., **Listening to Reason**,
1986; **Art for Other People No 20**,
1986; **Heart and Mind**, 1986;
Art for Other People No 21, 1986;
Tooth and Claw, 1985

own words) of his earlier sculpture, and at the same time provide for a different way of thinking about the autonomy of the sculptural object.

Significantly, in *Silence, Exile, Cunning*, Deacon situates his practice for the first time firmly within the shared social realm determined by language and he does so by metaphorizing the making of work by reference to the making of speech. 'Since speech is constitutive of ourselves as human', he writes, 'to speak is both to cause the world to be and to be oneself. At the same time, speech is not a thing, but rather it is a product of community, built bit by bit in discourse. Speech is not nature like stone or rock; it is manufactured. To make is also to bring into being, to cause there to be something'[4].

Even though in this short text, as elsewhere, there are real difficulties in the way in which Deacon deploys the language metaphor – drawing for example, even when it is developed into a systematic method, is no more capable of furnishing a grammar than speech – this short extract touches upon three central issues which are important to understanding his work thereafter.

Firstly, by making speech and, by implication, facture – the making of things – a fundamental attribute of human being; and by bringing the making of works of art within this general framework, Deacon is being careful to claim no more for the objects of art than for any other category of manmade thing. There is a strongly egalitarian under-tow to much of his thinking as an artist, and under this rubric, if under no other, he is insisting that works of art enjoy the same status in broadly human terms as newspapers, washing machines,

motorcars and buildings. They are all part and parcel of the one reflexive relationship – that of manufacture – linking the human subject to the world at large. Making the world present to us and ourselves present to the world. It could be that Deacon is guilty of a degree of over-statement here, since the world is present to us in a brute sense even if we do not speak about it or act upon it. But in terms of providing a construction of the work of art which has an unequivocal social dimension – which sees it as arising out of the complex, communicative fabric given to human societies – the point is well made. And this brings us to the second important issue.

Deacon makes it abundantly clear that he sees speech as the vital connective tissue of community. There is nothing exceptional about such a notion, nor is it unreasonable to argue that the making of things functions in a similar way. However, when he then describes spoken discourse as something 'built bit by bit' and goes on to claim that speech is 'manufactured', a curious and highly significant reversal occurs in the thrust of his metaphor.

Out of its very nature, spoken discourse is never unitary. Neither is it constructed piece-meal, sentence by sentence, in the manner of written language. It is a much more fluid and open-ended affair involving a whole range of different modes of physical communication. St. Augustine, in a quotation much loved by Ludwig Wittgenstein and used by him as the opening paragraph of *Philosophical Investigations*[5], puts it very neatly when he states that 'meaningful speech' is 'shown by body movements, as if it were the natural language of all peoples: the expression of the face, the play of the eyes, the movement of other parts of the body, and the tone of the voice which expresses our state of mind in seeking, having, rejecting and avoiding things'. Before all else, speech is a product of our bodylines, and the inherent human tendency to conviviality. Addressing a colloquium on 'Style'[6], Barthes, in a typically witty aside, described speech as a 'congregation of communicators' beyond the constraints of grammar and the reach of conventional linguistics: the congregational aspects of which 'remained to be described'. Just exactly how speech manages to convey clear and unambiguous meaning, then, is no simple matter. Texts are self-evidently additive, unitized assemblages of a linear kind, subject to the syntactical closure which meaningful sentences demand, and with a locus in the abstract space of the printed or written page. Speech, by contrast,

is more in the order of an 'incarnation' expanding and moving within the social space. Certainly it is not 'built' in any sense; neither is it 'manufactured'. In spoken discourse meaning resides as much in its disjunctions, its truncations and its dislocations – in a gesture of the hand, the involuntary twitch of a muscle or a barely perceptible flicker of the eye – as it does in those oral fragments which, in terms of grammar, happen to be glued together properly: the bits which make immediately transcribably, continuous sense. In this respect, speaking tends to reveal what writing purposefully seeks to hide: the complex and genuinely mysterious, ontological terrain out of which all meaning emerges – the place of language itself.

Viewed in this light we might be forgiven for concluding that writing is perhaps a more appropriate referent through which to discuss matters like 'building', 'manufacture' and the

Tell Me No Lies
1984
Galvanized steel, rivets
300 × 400 × 300 cm
Collection, FRAC des Pays de la
Loire, France

'making' of works of art. We might even be excused the suspicion that Deacon is guilty of making spoken discourse over again in the image of his own working practices. But this would be to mistake the serious purpose underlying his statement.

Later writings show Deacon to be very preoccupied with the problem of meaning. Most especially he argues against the two extremes of 'literal' and 'epistolary' meaning: meaning which subsists in a reification of the material facts of the work, as it arises, for instance, in Minimalist sculpture; and the meaning which depends on some kind of secondary text, validated through the person of the artist acting as a ghost author. What is also clear from Deacon's writings is that he wishes meaning to arise from within the bounds of social discourse, and for this he needs a theory of making which is closely tied to the workings of language. The critic and art historian Lynne Cooke, in her essay *Object Studies*[7] – a catalogue introduction to a series of works by Deacon grouped under the title 'Art for Other People' – quotes him, quoting Charles Harrison's book, *Empathy and Irony*.

Sculpture mediates and models a notion of what the world is like, a belief which owes much of its embodiment in language as its objecthood and its material identity.

Harrison is quite correct of course, but the simple fact of sculpture's 'embodiment' in language might not be considered sufficient guarantee of 'intentional' meaning.

Given that language is the very ground of social being, just how does a work of art – a sculpture in this case – in its specificity achieve common recognition as a 'model' of what the world is like? Is it, must it be, out of the artist's 'intention' to model the social world and to accept the burden of responsibility for embodying its meanings, or might it come about in some other way?

By temperament Deacon would most likely choose the path of intention and responsibility, but like many other artists of his generation who trouble themselves with this question, he can also see the pitfalls that lie in wait along the way. If we are to take on board the general thrust of his metaphor we must conclude that he is particularly afraid of the kind of closure which the intention 'to mean' demands: the punctum; the terminus; the fullstop. Above all he wishes to reserve a space for innovation, and here we can see clearly why he chooses to link the making of sculpture with speaking rather than with writing. In spoken discourse meaning is always open to negotiation, and negotiation, in its turn, serves to situate innovation – the making of new meanings – firmly within the social domain. For Deacon, the space in which meanings are made is a communal space, and the artist's relations to it is an ethical one. It is the very opposite of that free-wheeling space – playground of the ego – in which the artist rehearses and celebrates what Charles Altieri has described as 'the metaphysics of an assumed marginality'[8].

And this brings us to the third key issue raised by this fragment of Deacon's 'Orpheus' text: the problem of 'being'.

Some ten years later, in an interview with the Yugoslavian critic Marjetica Potrc published in

Tall Tree in the Ear
1983-84
Galvanized steel, laminated wood,
canvas
308 × 105 × 205 cm

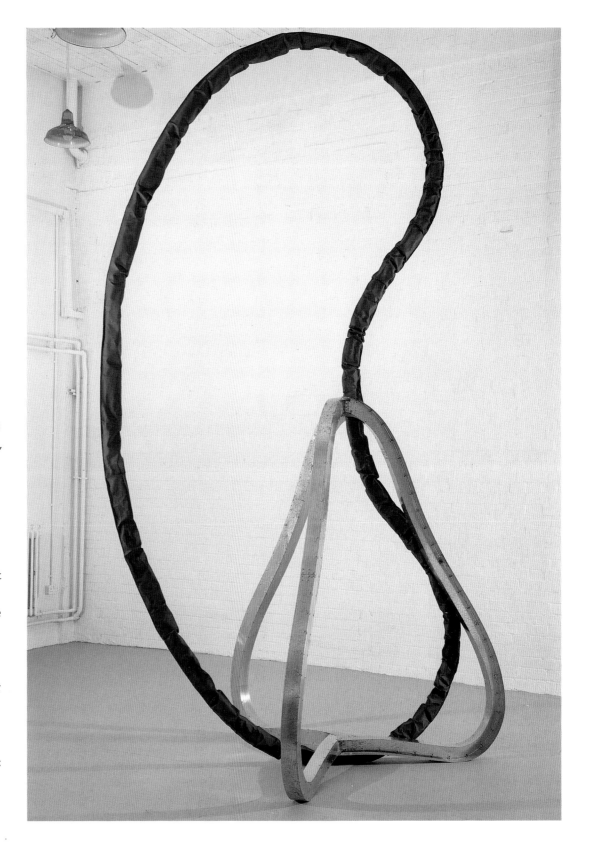

M'ARS magazine [9], Deacon seems to take a very
negative position in relation to the idea of 'being'.
After a brief discussion on meaning in which he
argues that the Minimalists, far from solving the
problems of meaning, had only postponed it, he
goes on to discuss the experience of the work of
art and the relationship of experience to meaning.
He praises the Minimalists for having got rid of
the 'essentialist' notions associated with high
abstraction, and states that for him the question
of meaning is not about identifying the essence
of the work with a metaphysical experience like
'being' and that he tends to view such experiences
as 'contextual rather than absolute'. There appears
to have been a very significant shift in his thinking,
then, from the time that he made the Orpheus
drawings and wrote the commentary *Silence,
Exile, Cunning*.

    Closer examination, however, shows that this
shift is not as great as it first appears. Under the
sway of Rilkian poetics Deacon was unavoidably
caught up with the question of 'being', and not just
human 'being' or the 'being' of things in the world.
The very first stanza of *Sonnets to Orpheus* sets the
metaphysical tone of Rilke's whole enterprise:

   A tree ascending. O pure transcension!
   O Orpheus sings! O tall tree in the ear!
   All noise suspended, yet in that suspension what
   a new beginning, beckoning, change, appear![10]

Transcendence, transubstantiation, suspension,
the apparition of change; this is the stuff and
vocabulary of a metaphysical experience of 'being':
the idea that there is something above, beyond or
outside of material circumstances; that matter
might be rendered ethereal, or vice versa; that the

passage of time can be slowed down or even stopped and the exact moment of change – '"being" in the process of becoming' as Plato called it – directly apprehended in the form of a ghostly intimation of a different order of existence. Such notions are the meat of Rilke's poetic vision, and it is hard to imagine a close involvement with the Sonnets of the kind which Deacon describes, which at the same time rejects all of this. Nevertheless, it is possible to detect a certain wariness on Deacon's part as early as the Orpheus commentary.

It shows itself in a confusion or a reluctance to confront certain very difficult questions with regard to the constellation of meaning and representation with autonomy. Writing about the Orpheus drawings in his notebooks[11] he says, for example, 'the drawings are intentionally extremely representational' but that he has 'difficulty in deciding of what they are representations'. And the passage continues: 'This concerns their reference. I have difficulty in corroborating their reference with something. Except I have considered *Sonnets to Orpheus* to be their subject'.

The question which is struggling to surface here is unmistakably that of the work of art's autonomy. How does the intention to represent something square with the desire for autonomy in the work of art? How does the work of art come to represent something other than itself and at the same time remain nothing but itself? And, more pointedly, precisely what order of experience does autonomy represent?

Deacon's preferred solution is to interject the works themselves – in this case the finished drawings – into the space between his intention to represent something and the specificity of the subject – *Sonnets to Orpheus* – in the belief that a representation might, will, has occurred, which in no way depends upon the particularities of the thing represented. It is rather like saying that you can paint a portrait of someone without referring at all to their physical appearance; and so you can, but only by recourse to things invisible. The painting would have to refer to the 'spirit', 'Psyche' or 'being' of that person, where 'being' is manifest through qualities other than their physical characteristics. Picasso's retort when Gertrude Stein complained that her portrait looked nothing like her, comes to mind: 'No, but one day you will look like it'. From Picasso's point of view he had been concerned to represent the 'essential' Gertrude Stein rather than Gertrude Stein as she appeared in front of him. He therefore regarded his portrait to be more 'true' than one based on appearances.

But Deacon is clearly very reluctant to resort to this kind of explanation. As he readily admits, for him it is one thread in a knot of theoretical questions which he finds very difficult to untie. He wishes to retain a more or less strong version of the autonomy of the sculptural object without having to ground this autonomy in a metaphysical alterity like 'being' and 'otherness'. He wants his work to be implicitly meaningful rather than 'textual': and he wants to hold on to the possibility of intentional representation without the sculptures themselves being shaped in any obvious way by what they represent.

In practice Deacon bridges this theoretical lacuna by recourse to two key working principles:

Stuff Box Object
1970-71
Performance work

the belief that work itself – his engagement with the processes and means of manufacture – is its own guarantee of meaning; and that both representation and autonomy are realized in, are determined by and in relationship to context. The model he uses to achieve this theoretical bridging is a theory of language, and here something of a contradiction emerges. Deacon's approach to language seems to bare some of the hallmarks of a phenomenological way of thinking, and in phenomenology the question of language is closely tied to the question of 'being'.

Viewed in the light of Deacon's early student background, the most intellectually formative period of which was in the sculpture department at St. Martin's School of Art between 1969 and 1972, this trace of phenomenological thinking is in no way surprising. At St. Martin's, Deacon worked in what was known as the 'A' course; a course which had been set up to provide an alternative way of thinking about sculpture to the prevailing ethos of the department: the perception-based, formal approach of Anthony Caro and the younger 'New Generation' sculptors. The 'A' course employed 'behaviourist' teaching methods, and encouraged the students to adopt a critical, even a sceptical attitude towards traditional notions of sculpture-making. The result was a wide variety of process-based sculptural work, ranging from performances to object-making which used materials as part of an 'event-structure' to arrive at a completed form. Integral to the teaching of this course was an approach to thinking which went beyond the normal boundaries of art historical and critical material into selective areas of general philosophy,

linguistics and psycho-analytical theory. Certain writers and texts were from time to time deemed de rigueur, amongst them Edward Giffin's *Logical Atomism*, Edmund Husserl's *Phenomenology of Perception*, as well as books by more fashionable writers like Marshall McLuhan, Edward de Bono and R.D. Lang[12]. The approach taken to this material was by no means systematic, rather it served to institute a climate of discourse with its own very distinctive vocabulary.

In this milieu Deacon was engaged mainly with performance work, albeit performance which had a strongly material-based aspect to it. This was the time of *Stuff Box Object*, 1971, a work which developed through several different stages (see page 110); starting its life as part of a communal student project, progressing through a performance phase – during which Deacon took up a foetal position, working inside the box – and ending up as a process-based sculptural object. As the critic Michael Newman has pointed out, *Stuff Box Object* initiates many of the issues and themes which surface in a different way in Deacon's later work, in particular, 'it looked forward to the way in which the sculpture was to become both a literal object and a metaphorical substitute for the person'[13], an aspect of Deacon's work we will need to return to later.

At this time too, Deacon was reading widely in the field of general linguistics and in his last year at St. Martin's wrote a paper linking language with perception, or to be more precise 'speaking' with 'looking' by way of description[14]. A notion which is not far removed from the phenomenological term 'self-showing'[15], part of phenomenology's tendency

In Two Minds No 2
1986
Galvanized steel, carpet
275 × 405 × 305 cm
Collection, Stedelijk Museum,
Amsterdam

to 'linguifaction'[16]: turning the world into language.

More generally, the period of Deacon's studentship at St. Martin's and his continued involvement afterwards with the studio-based performance group 'Many Deed' was a time of intense material and procedural experimentation as well as searching examination of himself and the social world, including the nature and purpose of works of art. It was already apparent that he was gifted with great practical intelligence: his hands had little difficulty in accomplishing what his mind thought. At St Martin's he was encouraged to challenge this facility and also to think in more radical ways about the possibilities of sculpture as an interventionary practice. Even so, in the midst of all this questioning and experimenting, concerns began to be established which were to surface in a different form in his mature work. Two are worth

mentioning here: a fascination with the way in which materials behave when they are subjected to repetitive forming processes; and an obsessive preoccupation with the unfamiliar, or more precisely, with defeating in himself the 'denial' which the unfamiliar often provokes. In this respect, a piece like *Speak/Work Performance*, performed by 'Many Deed' in 1974, out of the way in which it used routine, repetition, disruption and play-back, might be considered as something of a model for the formal games and strategies of making which Deacon engages with in his later work. Writing in the Tate Gallery catalogue in 1983 he says of his working method: 'I work with materials in the most straightforward way. I do not make plans. The activity is repetitious … I begin by shaping stuff … I may have something in mind or I may not. There are often radical changes. The unexpected happens. I am never sure whether I finish the thing I am making or whether it finishes with me'.

Underlying these staccato, seemingly very direct statements is a conception of sculpture as both practice and object of a highly provocative, even a revolutionary kind, and it has its origin in the event structure aspect of performance work. It opposes the 'occasion of making' against the more traditional notion of a pre-emptive creative vision; 'serialized fabrication' against ideated sculptural form; 'repetitive action' against original intuition; and the 'condition of possibility' against the intention to reach a particular kind of sculptural conclusion.

To return briefly to the Orpheus text. As we have already observed, there is an important side to Deacon's thinking which seeks to hold the making of works of art within the scope and reach of a definition of 'normal' human activity. And to this end he invokes the generic category of 'things manufactured'.

Manufacture, the making of things, he argues – and here he means all making, machine-made as well as hand-crafted items; consumer durables as well as sculptural objects – is to 'cause something', it is to 'bring it into being'. Once again, as a generalization, the statement is beyond argument, just as long as we pay no special attention to his use of the term 'being'. If we put any weight at all on the word 'being' the import of Deacon's statement changes. No longer is it a straightforward description but a reference to the existential root of phenomenology as represented by the writings of Martin Heidegger [17]. Looked at from this point of view – and Deacon was reading Heidegger at about this time – it is reasonable to assume that he is implying more here than appears at first sight, and at the same time avoiding an important question of definition: just how do works of art differ from other manufactured things; in what sense might they be said to be special?

By making the metaphorical link between speaking and facture; in claiming that speech is man-made – he is careful to point out, remember, that it 'is not nature like stone or rock' – Deacon would seem to be giving tacit recognition to two and possibly three, quite distinct, notional categories of 'being': being in language; being in nature; and more obliquely, being in culture. These categories, of course, are not unrelated, on the contrary, our construction of the natural world as

well as the cultural, is made from within language, since language has no boundaries and so permits of no exterior space. In Heidegger's now classic formulation: 'Language does not need to be founded, for it is what founds' [18]. In this important respect, 'beingness', in as far as we are able to know it through language, is indeed, indivisible. All things, whether natural or man-made, are incorporated into the work and 'being' of language. All things partake in what Michel Foucault has called the 'illusionary inwardness' of language – our subjectivity – and the process of reconciliation this demands of us vis à vis our experience of the external world. But this is to speak of language only on the ontological level: it is to speak of Language with a capital 'L'; the foundational terrain which allows 'languages' to become intelligible one to another. And viewed from this site, to 'bring into being' is neither more or less than to 'bring to consciousness'. The question of how things come into consciousness, how they describe themselves to us – in which particular language or by what manner of usage – is the critical one. Indeed, it is not overstating the case to say that it is this aspect of language which provides the essential ground for the hermeneutic work of all changing and lively cultures.

Ludwig Wittgenstein in the posthumously published fragments Zettel, touches upon this question when he writes: 'Do not forget that a poem, even though it is composed in the language of information, is not used in the language game of giving information' [19]. A poem by Sylvia Plath, then, though it uses the same lexicon and rules of grammar as a Government circular explaining how

to go about claiming housing benefit, by the way in which it engages with language declares itself to be absolutely other to it. It deploys the panoply of linguistic means differently and for palpably different ends.

As Michel Foucault has argued, although as human beings we are possessed of the strong impression that language is internal to us – an interior faculty of some kind by means of which we negotiate our relationship with the external world – in fact the opposite is the case. Language starts from outside with the world of real things. The word is as much an object as the thing or state of affairs to which it refers, free to detach and relocate itself within new configurations of meaning, and poetic rhetoric depends crucially upon this mobility. The possibility of using many words for the same object; several expressions to describe the same mood or state of mind; new and different ways of speaking about ordinary things such as will lift them into the realm of the extraordinary, is the necessary precondition of the poetic text. Poetry works with, indeed it is a celebration of this arbitrariness in language. While the functional, communicative, administrative text closes down the space between the sign and the signified, seeks to preserve the illusion of a necessary relatedness on behalf of objectivity or clarity, the poetic text opens it up, uses it as a site for the play of individual subjec-tivity in writer and reader alike. Where the rhetoric of the instrumental text pretends a fixed relation between words and world, poetic rhetoric sees this relation as one which must be forged over and over again in the engine of the individual imagination.

To bring the example closer to home, and in a more complex form. Deacon, who in his notebooks describes himself as a 'fabricator', uses the language – forms, configurations and methods of making and building – we tend to associate with processes of manufacture, technical engineering, furniture construction and industrial pattern-making. His sculptures derive their surface detail from these various processes, which results in a complicated play of what he called 'resonance' and 'equivalence'[20]. They resonate other levels of meaning and refer analogously to other things in the world. At the same time they have a strong sense of identity as autonomous works of art. A work like *Blind, Deaf and Dumb*, for example, one of the two related works made for his Serpentine Gallery exhibition of 1985, looks very much like a piece of industrial ducting; *More Light,* 1987-88, has the appearance of an abandoned piece of space technology; and the sardonically titled *Never Mind*, commissioned for the Middelheim sculpture park, Antwerp (Belgium) and installed in 1993, looks like a huge wooden former of the kind that might be used to spin a large metal vessel or panel-beat something like an engine-housing. However, while they might be said to resemble certain familiar things – while they seem to make connection with objects that we know from other contexts – they do not represent them in a straightforward way. Deacon's use of the term 'equivalence', in as far as it seems to suggest a hyphenation of the word 'representation', is important here. His sculptures tend to 're-present' carefully selected aspects of familiar things as a part of their linguistic array rather than serving to specify the sculpture as a singular representation. 'Equivalences', in this respect, are not authorized directly by the artist, but authorize themselves in the mind of the viewer as a transaction in language. Furthermore, these resemblances or 'equivalences' as Deacon calls them are a function of only one kind of language deployed in the making of the sculpture; we might describe it as a technical or instrumental language. And this in turn is overlaid upon another very different kind of language. This second language we might call 'poetic' language since it is centrally concerned with the aesthetic play of material manipulation and material forms. The ruggedness and immediacy which often characterizes the working of poetic language in Deacon's sculptures – the feeling that they have been wrestled into existence rather more quickly than their scale or detailing would permit – gives to them their very distinctive charge.

To some degree these languages displace and modify each other. The technical language enters the aesthetic domain as a mark of excess; as a decorative overload. And this surplus of technical detail, in turn, serves to de-sublimate the aesthetic and formal aspects of the work, returning it to and holding it firmly within the bounds of human labour. We could describe this transaction as a redistribution of language, a transmigration of

characteristic usages, and in some respects this is precisely what it is. But it is also important to recognize that this is not a simple homogenizing process. The result is never a true amalgam. Redistribution happens across a gap, a fault-line which draws into itself the viewing subject as an active agent in the making of meaning. Most importantly, it is in this linguistic gap that the identity of the object as a work of art – rather than any other kind of manufactured thing – is first negotiated. At the heart of this exchange, the pivot around which this double play of languages is organized, there lies a characteristic argument about the nature of sculptural form. We might describe it as a dialectic between inside and outside as well as between volumetric, spatial structure and what Deacon calls 'lump': the solid, fully rounded, no-nonsense sculptured object.

As we have already remarked, reading Rilke's sonnets and making the Orpheus drawings started Deacon thinking in a new way about the autonomy of sculpture. The works exhibited at The Gallery on Acre Lane immediately prior to his trip to America[21] seemed to be studiedly earth-bound, their form ponderous in its construction and static in the way in which it engaged with space. The several untitled works which followed his return from the States had a very different feel to them. They enjoyed a more active relationship with the floor and with the space in which they stood. Indeed, *Untitled*, 1980, a large, curvilinear, open structure made of laminated strips of plywood jointed with steel, might be considered a seminal work since it manifests many of the procedural characteristics which Deacon returns to over and over again in the

Installation, The Gallery, Brixton,
London
1978
top, l. to r., **Untitled**, 1978;
Untitled, 1975; **Untitled**,
1977-78

bottom, l. to r., **Untitled**, 1976,
Untitled, 1977; **Untitled**,1975

Like a Bird
1984
Laminated wood
Approx. 300 × 600 × 500 cm

Never Mind
1993
Wood, stainless steel, epoxy
310 × 765 × 300 cm
Installed, Middelheim Sculpture
Park, Antwerp

Untitled
1980
Laminated wood
300 × 289.6 × 289.6 cm

years that follow. It is the first truly open form. It has its own very specific brand of formal integrity. While it sits upon the ground it does not seem to have been built in relationship to it: rather it seems to spring from it. Taken together these qualities make it the genuine precursor of the other great laminated works; pieces like *For Those Who Have Ears*, 1983; *Blind, Deaf and Dumb*, 1985; *Double Talk*, 1987; and *Breed*, 1989.

But this early work, *Untitled*, 1980, is significant for another and perhaps more important reason: it seems to have inaugurated the dialectic of inside and outside in a new way. The work implies a closure but is also possessed of a strong invitational aspect, reaching out and beckoning the spectator to enter its interior space. The possibility of effecting such an entrance is signalled by a tear-shaped opening – it is almost a schematically drawn vagina. Negotiation between inside and outside is given a distinctly erotic edge, an edge which allows us to approach the question of 'being' from a different direction.

Eros is unmistakably present when 'being' and 'other' are brought into a particular geometry of relationship. It might be described as both a 'coming together' and a 'holding apart'; a proximity in which a distance is integrally maintained. The deep pathos which Eros commands is made up of

Untitled
1980

For Those Who Have Ears No 2
1983
Laminated wood
274 × 366 × 153 cm
Collection, Tate Gallery, London

this closeness and this duality. Immanuel Levinas describes this alterity with great precision by means of the linked and hyphenated phrases, 'being-in-one's-skin, having-the-other-in-one's-skin' [22]. The comma stands between, binds together and holds apart. The skin, as container, becomes a site for oscillation and substitution.

With Eros in tow, then, 'bringing into being' goes beyond mere cognition; beyond the selfish pleasure we routinely derive from sensible exchange with things in the world – our own 'being' is implicated. Deacon himself remarks upon this kind of dynamic substitution in an interview with the curator Julian Heynen. The spectator, he suggests, is 'in the position of feeling occasionally outside and occasionally inside the sculpture ... the feeling of being engulfed by the object you are looking at does change the subject/object relationships ... one has the sense of becoming, on occasion, the object of the sculpture as much as the sculpture is object for you' [23]. 'Engulfed' – taken over by, submerged within – seems to suggest more than a simple switching of the relationship between subject and object: it suggests a dissolving of the distinction altogether. Certainly it proposes a state of being with the work that cannot be encompassed by a term like 'looking at'.

Another way in which Deacon describes this alternating relationship between the sculpture and the viewer is as 'private engagement' and he qualifies this by adding 'as if with another person' [24]. Furthermore he attributes this kind of intimate 'engagement' to the larger sculptures

following pages, **Double Talk**
1987
Laminated wood
245 x 855 x 305 cm

Breed
1989
Laminated hardboard, aluminium,
screws
2 parts, 150 × 520 × 300 cm
overall
Collection, Centre Georges
Pompidou, Paris

These Are the Facts
1987-88
Hardboard, mild steel, carpet,
phosphor bronze
200 × 195 × 133 cm

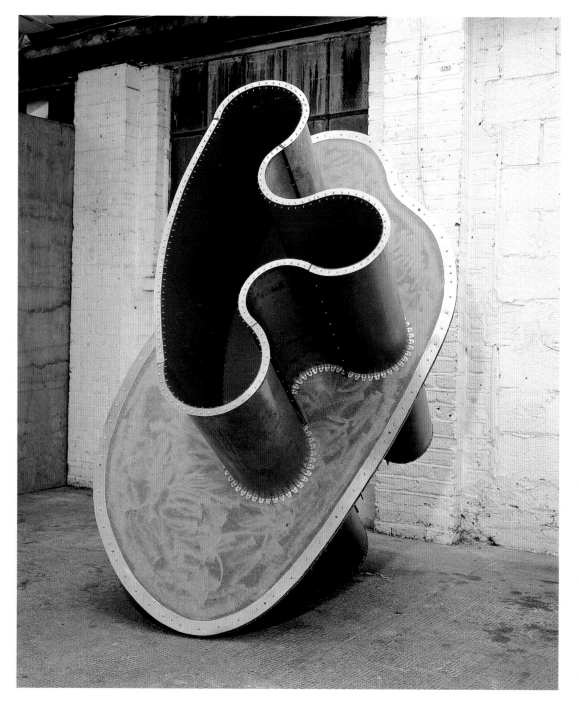

rather than the smaller works which comprise the *Art for Other People* series. The experience offered by these works is more 'public' and has something of the quality of a 'conversation' about it. Once again 'engagement' seems to suggest some kind of encapsulation, a loosing of the self to the work, a wrapping up of the subject/object duality within an experience of solitude; while 'conversation' proposes a more open and objective relationship taking place as part of the discourse of community. This seeming reversal of our expectations with regard to public and private space raises another fascinating question in the domain of language. Is the language of 'engagement' occasioned by the large sculptures the same as that inaugurated as 'conversation' by the smaller ones, and if not, in what sense might it be said to be different? And more pointedly: given the alterity of erotic substitution which characterizes our 'engagement' with the larger pieces, does connective, communally constitutive language enter into the equation at all, or are we in the presence of an entirely different order of discourse?

Significantly, the notion of autonomy in the Orpheus story finds its most powerful representation in the image of Orpheus' decapitation. His head is torn from his body while he is still speaking, and it continues to speak even after it has been thrown into the river. Indeed, Orpheus' voice remains audible long after his head has floated out of sight. Eurydice, the subject of his adoration and his lamentation, has long since shaded away into the gross darkness of the underworld. To whom then is Orpheus' severed head addressing itself and on whose behalf?

top left,
Art for Other People No 1
1982
Stone, leather
30 × 90 × 30 cm

top right,
Art for Other People No 7
1983
Linoleum, galvanized steel
13 × 52 × 13 cm

bottom left,
Art for Other People No 2
1982
Marble, wood, vinyl, resin
43 × 158 × 33 cm

bottom right,
Art for Other People No 6
1983
Suede, brass
25 × 45 × 25 cm

right,
Art for Other People No 9
1983
Galvanized steel, rivets
53 × 34 × 11 cm

Survey   64

Surely in this brutally separated, continuously vocal head, song, speech, language itself is quite literally disembodied. The voice is driven by its own momentum into the beyond of language, to the outer reaches of reality, to the very edge of the unreal, and there, separated from the community of bodies, it becomes its own delicate affirmation. In this utterly 'other' place, the head speaks sweetly to itself in its own tongue. It has only to convince itself of the truth of its own descriptions: it has only to persuade itself of the validity of those sadnesses and delights which animate its inner world. Thus it is that Orpheus' decapitation represents an extreme form of autonomy within the domain of language: the possibility of an utterance which is 'of' and 'for' itself; a retreat from the language as a routing affirmation of community into the solitary space of one's own 'being'.

The disembodiment which entrance into this solitary place implies is precisely that of an 'engagement' in which the duality of subject and object, the distinction between 'self' and the 'other', is dissolved. From within, this solitude has the appearance of the absolute, but in reality its offer is, in the very strictest sense, that of an 'engagement' which in turn necessitates a 'dis-engagement': we can enter it and leave it at will. It is in this respect the opposite of 'conversation'. Conversations begin and end; they are interrupted or they are concluded. Either way they are sufficient unto themselves; they carry with them no promise of continuity. 'Engagement' by contrast, suggests that there is always something there to be engaged with, something to return to; a different order of discourse, a different quality of experience. And because engagement is instigated in solitude it can only be shared paradigmatically. We might all have the same experience, but the attribution of 'sameness' can never be tested without recourse to the guarantee afforded by common language and common usage. The encapsulation which 'engagement' works with gives no such guarantee and needs none, so intense is the experience it provides.

Deacon's larger sculptures exercise a very different version of sculptural presence to the smaller works which comprise the *Art for Other People* series. In part, this is out of intention: Deacon intends the small works to function differently; he intends them to occupy the world in a more matter-of-fact way. Lynne Cooke, in her catalogue essay introducing these works, puts it very succinctly when she writes: 'In these small pieces Deacon can be said to be proposing a singular alternative to the homeless state endemic to much modernist sculpture, undermining the social isolation of sculpture as a fine art by seeking out spaces in which the discourse of high art is traditionally absent'[25]. But Deacon's intention to difference is only part of the story. There is something about the way in which he uses scale in conjunction with different strategies of making, which brings the larger sculptures more into the domain of bodily sensation than mental apprehension. Addressing sculptural objects we tend in any case to 'look at' small things and 'look into' larger ones – where 'into' might be taken to mean a peripatetic investigation as well as the movement into or through something. In Deacon's case this 'looking into' is greatly enhanced by the

opposite
top left,
Art for Other People No 10
1984
Galvanized steel, linoleum
40 × 90 × 90 cm

top right,
Art for Other People No 13
1984
Stainless steel, linoleum
47 × 96.5 × 9 cm

bottom left,
Art for Other People No 12
1984
Marble, leather
42 × 35 × 20 cm

bottom right,
Art for Other People No 17
1985
Galvanized steel, linoleum
122 × 152.5 × 46 cm

opposite, Installation,
Kunstverein Hannover, 1993
background, **What Could Make Me
Feel This Way A**
1993
Bent wood with glue, screws,
cable ties
286 × 560 × 483 cm
Collection, Sprengel Museum,
Hannover
foreground, **What Could Make Me
Feel This Way B**
1993
Stainless steel
2.5 × 630 × 315 cm

**What Could Make Me Feel This
Way A**
1993
Pencil, ballpoint pen on graph
paper
21 × 30 cm

way in which he fabricates his work: the studied use of open form as in the elaborately constructed *What Could Make Me Feel This Way A*, 1993; and forms which are self-evidently not solid but are built as a skin, of which the most dramatic example is *Struck Dumb* made in 1988. Even when he chooses to use solid form as with *Distance No Object No 2*, 1989, the mass or 'lump' as Deacon calls it is constructed from the inside out, and its exterior surface – its skin – functions as a graphic record, a mapping of its internal complexities. In one way or another, all of Deacon's larger sculptures describe and articulate an interior space and by doing so invite a particular kind of 'interjection' on the part of the spectator. The viewer is required to make an imaginary journey into the interior of the work, and once this process of 'interjection' has occurred,

once the viewer has taken possession of this interior, then the inrush of contextual material is held at bay and a state of identification is achieved which is more physical than linguistic. As it is with the inward experience of our own body, the viewer is in an important sense 'unvoiced'. Once inside, there is no 'other', there is no one to speak to, no one to hear. Paradoxically, if we are to describe this experience of inwardness, we must first of all withdraw from it, and this act of withdrawal is a withdrawal 'into' the world of constitutive language. For this reason the adequacy of our description must always be in doubt.

We have already touched upon the way in which Deacon's sculpture utilizes the interface between two very different languages – the instrumental and the poetic – and shown how the

opposite and following pages,
**What Could Make Me Feel This
Way A**
1993

opposite, **Distance No Object No 2**
1989
Aluminium, glass fibre
163 × 300 × 101 cm
Collection, Museet for
Samtidskunst, Oslo

left, **Struck Dumb**
1988
Welded mild steel with bolts
157 × 392 × 266 cm
Collection, Tate Gallery, London

Dummy
1992
Wood
51 × 311 × 178 cm
Collection, Auckland City Art
Gallery, New Zealand

identity of the object as a work of art is first negotiated in the gap which opens up between the two. The play between 'inside' and 'outside', so characteristic of Deacon's work in as far as it asks a fundamental question about the efficacy of language to deal with all aspects of our experiencing works of art, tends to function as another, similar kind of alterity. This time it is inescapably an alternating movement between 'being' and 'other': between the eroticized, undifferentiated site of desire – the 'before', if you like, the desire has been put into words – and the social world as it is shaped by and through the intricate play of different languages. Surface detail, the skin and the metaphorizing of the sculpture as body allows for an outwardly inflected reading as well as an inwardly inflected one. The former, by its nature, is highly conventionalized. It is a reading, embedded in context and subject to the normative experiences which context offers. In this sense it serves chiefly to reinforce the notion of sculpture as a public transaction. The latter, the inwardly inflected state of reading, is emptied of customary meanings; it yields up no comfortable assumptions about world, self, or other. Reading occurs in an anachronic space in which the only consistency is an inconstant self and the welter of desires which self represents. But it is important to emphasize that these two types of identification are experienced as an alterity and not as an opposition. Levinas' formulation, 'being-in-one's-skin, having-the-other-in-one's-skin', describes a two-way passage between 'inside' and 'outside'; one that allows for an inner experience of an outwardly apprehended 'other', and conversely, allows us to

project the intimate experience of 'being in and by oneself' into some 'other thing' situated in the outside world. This process of exchange is the root and ground of the work of art's autonomy.

While this pressing duality might be described as 'trans-physical', it need not necessarily amount to something 'metaphysical'. Certainly it does not depend upon the transcendent notion of 'being' of the kind that we find described in the opening stanzas of Rilke's *Sonnets to Orpheus*. But it does pose a radical question to the exclusive definition of the work of art, which makes it out to be con-structed entirely from within bounds set by socially constitutive languages. Indeed, it suggests that there is a relational aspect to our apprehension of things which precedes language both as a system and sign – in other words in the Barthian sense. If we are to take Barthes' idea of the 'music of meaning' seriously, then it can only be seen as something that we all carry with us as part of our baggage as sensible subjects. Meaning must then be 'caused', must arise out of desire, or, more precisely, out of the ontological joining of 'being' with language as it is first manifest in desire. Furthermore, the work of art must find its point of origin in this triangular constellation. It must speak on its behalf more or less directly and by doing so establish its absolute difference to all other 'manufactured' things.

Paradoxically, this idea that there is something in the presence of a work of art which stands in a problematic relation to the routine constructions of everyday language is signalled most clearly in the way in which Deacon uses titles. He chooses phrases which themselves are

Fish Out of Water
1986-87
Laminated hardboard
245 × 350 × 190 cm
Collection, Hirshhorn Museum and
Sculpture Garden, Washington D.C.

possessed of a high degree of autonomy – verbal asides, figures of speech, vernacular usages – which are immediately recognizable and have an independent, almost closed identity. Deacon's titles tend to produce a quality of silence around themselves. Almost they turn written language against itself through the deployment of a whole battery of closure devices: a rapid and irreversible slide from word into image (*Nose to Nose*); the use of onomatopoeia (*Struck Dumb, Double Talk*); tautological doubling (*Feast for the Eye*); cryptic nomination (*Breed*); self-referencing (*What Could Make Me Feel This Way, The Back of My Hand*); contradiction between word and image (*Like a Snail*); and personal asides (*O.T., The Interior Is Always More Difficult J.H.*). Not only do these devices allow the titles to stand to one side of the sculptures they name, but they isolate them in language too. Rather than qualifying the works verbally they function more like an appendix, an addendum or a footnote. They are neither essential to the apprehension of the sculpture nor do they serve to complete its meaning. In fact they occupy a different conceptual space altogether. Once again Deacon seems to be refusing to wrap things up, refusing homogenization. He is quite deliberately bringing things together and holding them apart at one and the same time. The conjoining of word with object is offered, but it must be negotiated by the viewer as a part of their engagement with the work: and this time the negotiation is between language and its 'other' – the 'before' of language – rather than one involving languages of different kinds.

Deacon's sculpture, then, works with two very different versions of autonomy. One, we might call

Kiss and Tell
1989
Epoxy, plywood, steel, timber
176 × 226 × 170 cm
Collection, Arts Council of Great
Britain, London

Lock
1990
Laminated hardboard, aluminium,
vinyl
242 × 382 × 301 cm
Collection, Weltkunst Foundation,
Zurich

'the autonomy of the Orphic head' and the other,
demonstrated clearly in the way in which he
attaches titles, we might describe as an erasure
of the background noise of language. The first of
these reveals itself through an attitude to forming
which denies even the vestiges of the secure
anchorage which, in its least disguised form,
figured historically as the plinth. In most cases
Deacon's sculptures consist of 'rolling' forms which
are shown in particular configurations but which
always carry with them the suggestion that they
might have fallen to the ground differently. This
quality is most apparent in a work like *Lock* made
in 1990. But it is also present to some degree in
the sculptures which are clearly built in relation to
the ground-plane, of which *Border*, 1991, is a good
example, or the more architectural *The Interior Is
Always More Difficult G* first exhibited at the Lisson
Gallery in 1992. In both cases the turning of the
base-edge of the work proposes an independence
or even a separation from the ground which is
entirely opposite to the causal, gravitational
relationship which governs most sculpture. The
second form of autonomy is one of nomination:
privileging certain carefully selected words or
phrases in such a way as to detach them from
customary patterns of language and usage, thereby
creating a 'meaningful' silence around them which
allows them to be floated across the gap between
language and object. The initial separation in both
of these strategies occurs in relation to context.
One gives the sculpture as object something of
the character of an event, the surprising nature of
which subsists in its sense of something having just
occurred in this place and no other. The other – the

The Back of My Hand No 5
1986
Galvanized steel, mixed media
250 × 150 × 20 cm

**The Interior Is Always More
Difficult G**
1992
Aluminium, polycarbonate
239 × 350 × 50 cm

Border
1991
Wood, welded PVC
48 × 335 × 171 cm
Collection, Fonds National d'Art
Contemporain, Paris

nominative – casts the sculpture as an emergence,
a coming into focus as a bearer of specific meaning,
detached from the general flux of meaning given
by language.

This insistence upon the play between the
sculpture as object and name, and context as an
interactive social space, sets Deacon very much
apart from the rest of the sculptors of his own
generation. Most especially it has provided him
with real social and philosophical grounds for
intervening in the public space and the large-scale.
Publicly commissioned works like *Nose To Nose,
Beginning To End* made for the Glasgow Garden
Festival in 1988, and *Moor*, 1990 commissioned for
the Victoria Park bridge Plymouth, as part of the
Four Cities, 'New Work for Different Places' project,
take the idea of public sculpture far beyond that of
the decorative addition to plaza architecture.

Deacon's public works function as a real and
highly provocative intervention in relationship both
to architecture and landscape. They are not easy
on the eye, neither do they carry the affirmation
of the monument. They tend to focus more upon
issues arising out of the context itself, to function
contrapuntally in relationship to factors like social
dereliction and urban decay.

Deacon has been described as the inheritor
of the tradition of British sculpture represented
historically by Barbara Hepworth and Henry
Moore, and his increasing involvement in public
commissions has contributed to this attribution.
But we can see from what has gone before that
this connection is at best superficial and at worst
downright misleading. His work stands very much
apart from the tradition of high abstraction

Moor
1990
Painted mild steel
500 × 247.5 × 350 cm
Commissioned for TSWA Four Cities
Project
Installed, Victoria Park, Plymouth

far left, **Naum Gabo**
Spiral Theme (Penetrated Version)
1937-40
Bronze
Collection, Tate Gallery, London

left, **Barbara Hepworth**
Conoid, Sphere and Hollow II
1937
Marble

espoused by Hepworth, and in radical opposition to the 'picturesque', nature-focused abstraction we associate with Moore. If there is a link to be made, it is best negotiated through the influence on British sculpture of the constructivist Naum Gabo. Like Deacon, Gabo was interested in a wide range of different discourses bridging the gap between art and science: philosophy; mathematics; architecture; design; and most especially advances in the social and natural sciences. And these interests helped shape the conceptual ground as well as the material look of his work. Like Deacon also, there is a clear dialectic of contrasting languages at work in Gabo's objects linking the poetic with the technical: a very refined 'sensual' side to the work and a more rigorous 'hard' side. In this respect, a sculpture like *Spheric Theme (Penetrated Variation)* worked on by Gabo over a three year period in the early sixties, in its attitude to the making of sculptural form and by the way in which Gabo opens up the centre of the form bears some comparison with a Deacon work like *Body of*

Thought, 1988, or with *Under My Skin* made in 1990. Gabo's *Red Stone*, 1964-65 seems to share some of the sculptural concerns addressed by Deacon in works like *Skirt*, 1989, and *Coat*, 1990. There are some grounds for connecting him with the constructive lineage of modern sculpture as it is represented by a figure like Gabo – certainly Deacon would identify closely with Gabo's much quoted dictum, 'the images man constructs determine the shape of the universe about us'. Furthermore the early influence of artists like Phillip King and more especially William Tucker, who himself taught alongside the British constructivist Kenneth Martin at Goldsmith's College prior to his time at St. Martin's, might be seen as reinforcing this connection. However, we must be careful not to tie his work into it too directly. Constructivism is pre-eminently a part of the Modernist, scientific utopian view.

Deacon, on the other hand, is quintessentially the postmodern artist. He belongs to no tendency or movement. He shares no stylistic concerns even

Nose to Nose, Beginning to End
1988
2 steel parts on concrete base
160 × 190 × 120 m
Installation, Glasgow Garden
Festival

Body of Thought No 2
1988
Aluminium, cardboard, galvanised
steel, copper, rivets
248 × 300 × 258 cm
Collection, Museum van
Hedendaagse Kunst, Antwerp

with the British sculptors of his own generation: Tony Cragg, Anish Kapoor, Bill Woodrow, Richard Wentworth and the rest. It is intrinsic to the condition of Postmodernity that artists, freed from the progressive, programmatic aspect of Modernism, are at liberty to choose their own style. Nowhere was this freedom of choice more clearly demonstrated than at the re-opening of the Middelheim sculpture park in Antwerp, when Deacon was shown alongside five other European sculptors who, with the exception of the Belgian artist Panamarenko, were of his own generation: the Spanish sculptor Juan Muñoz; the Germans Harald Klingelholler and Thomas Schütte, and the Danish painter and sculptor Per Kirkeby. At the level of content there were connections to be made. For example, Deacon might be said to share an interest in the interface between technology and the natural sciences with Panamarenko; a concern for language with Klingelhöller and Schütte; an interest in architecture with Kirkeby; an intention to activate social space with Schütte and Muñoz. But these shared interests manifest themselves in radically different sculptural forms. There is no evidence of a collegiate working method or sculptural style. There is no over-arching idea about what art or more particularly sculpture should be or looks like. The climate of ideas he inhabits is very much after structuralism and after what has been called 'the linguistic turn' in modern philosophy. If he were to believe in utopia at all, it would most likely be a utopia of the Barthian kind, a utopia of discourse. If he were to permit himself to dream, it would be a Barthian dream in which the fragmentation which characterizes contemporary

Installation, Galleria Locus Solus,
Genoa
1990
foreground, **Under My Skin**, 1990
background, **Band of Gold**, 1990

Cover
1990
MDF, copper
182.8 × 335.2 × 122 cm
Collection, Akron Art Museum,
Ohio

below, **Thomas Schütte**
Casino
1990
Wood, acrylic, 25 gouache on
paper drawings
Table, 172 × 172 × 102 cm
Casino, 122 × 110 × 100 cm
Gouache drawings,
50 × 65 cm each

bottom, **Harald Klingelhöller**
Die Furcht verläßt ihren
Gegenstand und geht über in Hass
(Fear Leaves Its Object and Turns
into Hate)
1993
Installed, Open-Air Museum of
Sculpture Middelheim

culture would be dissolved into a unifying play of
language. More importantly, in the more specialized
context of contemporary art, Deacon is very much a
post-Minimal artist – using the term literally rather
than art historically – throughout his writings he
casts his work in a critical relationship to artists
like Carl Andre and Donald Judd. In some respects
he sees himself working to correct some of the
reductive errors of Minimalism, especially with
regard to its formal strictures and its endemic
'materialism'.

But Deacon's contribution to contemporary
sculpture goes a great deal further than can be
summed up by reference to a slender thread of art
historical argument. As we have seen he is first
and foremost a thinking artist who is determined
to keep a lot of difficult historical, social and
theoretical issues in play. He wishes to hold onto
the notion of sculpture as an exemplary practice
given to him out of its tradition and its history,
but he wants at the same time to maintain it as a
strong site for innovation. He sees it as part of his
responsibility as an artist to connect his practice
to the 'horizontal culture'[26], rather than being
content to sit comfortably within the protective
fold of a privileged discourse. Before all else he
wants to take account of the post-critical debate
without losing the sculpture as object to the
shifting sands of fashionable discursive practices.

Coat
1990
Welded plastic
122 × 213.3 × 182.8 cm

1   Roland Barthes, *The Rustle of Language*, Basil Blackwell, Oxford, 1986, title essay

2   Richard Deacon, Kunstverein Hannover, 1993. Catalogue appended Workbiography

3   ibid.

4   ibid.

5   Ludwig Wittgenstein, *Philosophical Investigations*, Basil Blackwell, Oxford, 1962

6   Roland Barthes, *Collected Papers*, University of Leiden, 1969

7   Lynne Cooke, *Richard Deacon*, catalogue essay, Whitechapel Art Gallery, London, 1988

8   Charles Altieri, 'The Dilemma of Modernity' conference paper, unpublished, University of Michigan, 1993

9   Marjetica Potrc, 'Interview', *M'ARS*, Ljubljana, Vol. II, no. 4, 1990

10 Rainer Maria Rilke, *Selected Works* Vol II, Trans. J.B. Leishman, Hogarth Press, London, 1980

11 *Richard Deacon*, Kunstverein Hannover, 1993

12 I was teaching at St. Martin's at the time and these are examples of the books that were passed around amongst the staff as well as the students.

13 *Richard Deacon*, Kunstverein Hannover, 1993

14 ibid.

15 Georg Wilhelm Friedrich Hegel, *Phenomenology of Spirit*, Trans. A. V. Miller, Oxford University Press, 1977

16 Stephen Mellville, *Philosophy Beside Itself*, Manchester University Press, 1986

17 Confirmed in a conversation with Richard Deacon

18 Martin Heidegger, *Poetry, Language, Thought*, Trans. A. Hofstadter Harper and Row, London, 1970

19 Ludwig Wittgenstein, *Zettel*, Basil Blackwell, Oxford, 1967

20 *Richard Deacon*, Kunstverein Hannover, 1993

21 ibid.

22 Immanuel Levinas, *The Levinas Reader*, Edit. S. Hand, essay 'Time and Other', Basil Blackwell, Oxford, 1989

23 *Richard Deacon*, Kunstverein Hannover, 1993

24 ibid.

25 Lynne Cooke, *Richard Deacon*, catalogue essay, Whitechapel Art Gallery, London, 1988

26 The term 'horizontal' culture used by the Italian political philosopher, Vincenzo Sparagna. It means the ground of social life as opposed to the mechanisms of cultural validation which he describes as 'vertical'.

Three Small Works
1990
Epoxy coated paper, steel tea tray

Skirt
1989
Galvanized steel
80 × 353 × 185 cm
Collection, Fundacion Caixa de
Pensiones, Barcelona

Contents

Interview Pier Luigi Tazzi in conversation with Richard Deacon, page 6. Survey Jon Thompson

Thinking Richard Deacon, Thinking Sculptor, Thinking Sculpture, page 36. Focus Peter Schjeldahl Deacon's Faith,

page 88. Artist's Choice Mary Douglas Purity and Danger, 1966, page 98. Artist's

Writings Richard Deacon Selections from Stuff Box Object, 1971-72, page 110. Artist's Statement, 1982, page 114.

Silence, Exile, Cunning, 1986-88, page 116. What Car? Correspondence with Lynne Cooke, 1992 page 120. What You See Is What

You Get, 1992, page 132. Design for Replacing, 1987, page 138. Design for Factory, 1993, page 139. Reading: a propos de Toni

Grand, 1993, page 140. Chronology page 144 & Bibliography, page 158.

'What's that, then? Is it ducting?' one man said to another in London in 1985. The questionable object was a metal sculpture that Richard Deacon was assembling outside the Serpentine Gallery. 'Nah,' the other man answered, 'it's art. Look at the way it's put together.'

Deacon told me happily of the overheard conversation. I used it in another essay I wrote about his work. Now having agreed to discuss a single piece of Deacon's – I have selected *Keeping the Faith* – I think again of a casual exchange that touches the heart of his sculptural poetic.

'What's this, then? A bunch of lattice?'

'Must be a form for something.'

'Looks like a jet engine.'

'A squashed sort of one.'

'It's not finished, whatever it is.'

'Can't be. Wants cladding.'

Keeping the Faith
1992
Beechwood, epoxy
75 × 175 × 170 cm

My imaginary flâneurs are less canny than Deacon's real ones. 'Art' is not an explanation that occurs to them. I made sure of it so I could hear them out.

Keeping the Faith (it is often wise to postpone contemplating Deacon's subtle titles, which reward rather than direct attentive looking) is a bentwood framework riddled with holes left by the screws that held it together for gluing. Its form is symmetrical on the left-right axes of its length and breadth while asymmetrical on the up-down axis of its height, which thus feels distorted ('squashed'). It does not look like a finished thing, but rather like the completed phase of a fabrication process.

The nearest word for the work's type of form is 'pod'. Viewed from the side, it might well evoke a jet engine – or a Janus-headed fish of the bottom-feeding variety that has an underslung mouth or a Janus-hooded racing car with an air-scoop grill. Wrecking these associations is the odd hump in the middle of its bottom. I can't relate this eruption to anything imaginably functional.

The crease along the top and the hump in the bottom of the piece make sense together if you picture a small symmetrical pod in some pliable material, such as clay, grasped evenly with the fingertips of both hands and squeezed. Your fingers would make the crease, your thumbs the hump. To think of this while looking at the sculpture is to trigger a scale shift, summoning the fantasy of a King Kong-sized manipulator.

Viewed from either end, the work presents the graphic outline of an oval pinched in the middle, a shape with a biological or caricatural air: a diagram of cells separating or the mouth of a comic-strip character crying 'Waaah!' Also suggested is a figure eight or the infinity sign. Anyone looking at photographs of *Keeping the Faith* might deem such graphic resemblances primary. But they are the last aspects one notes in the structure's actual presence, where the bent maple slats and oozing yellowish glue exert an imperious matter-of-factness.

As a framework, the piece might seem to anticipate a completed hollow object that is either solid-walled (if a mold were the next, still transitional stage) or clad in form-fitting sheets of anything from riveted metal to kite paper. It is impossible that the pod could become a merely component part of some other form or that any additions to it (on the outside, at least) would significantly alter its shape. You would not go to the trouble of perfecting those streamlined contours and then jam something else onto them.

The making of *Keeping the Faith*'s unknowable object has halted at the framework stage where any fabrication yields the maximum of information about itself. Think of a house that is under construction, when everything is in place except wallboard and siding. What you see is the total quiddity of 'house' minus the idea of what it is for: habitation. The next phase of work will humiliate the structure into amenity.

Keeping the Faith (detail)
1992

Before concentrating on the sculpture's literal makeup, I return to its evocation of a jet engine or a racing car, as something to keep in mind. The form says *whoosh*. It looks like a product of exhaustive testing in a wind tunnel. Justifying its immobility is just its Janus-facedness, incurring stalemate by trying to zoom off in opposite directions simultaneously. To marry itself to speed seems the work's narcissistic fixation. (Everything Deacon makes can seem self-obsessively preoccupied with some action or other that it is somehow prevented from performing.)

I am moved – ravished, really – by the sculpture's extravagant investment of exacting toil in the execution of a design that had to be smackdab perfect in advance. Did Deacon work the form out on a computer? I can picture webbed traceries of pixel light rotating this way and that on a screen, adjusted by the hummingbird of a cursor. Whatever the process, one stage of it was necessarily a set of terrifically precise plans and measurements that presumed extreme technical knowhow and discipline. This thought lends a complicated poignance.

What do we require physically of any sculpture, beyond that it not spontaneously fall apart? It seems to me an article of sophisticated taste, tested in the experimental history of modern art, that the minimum criterion of sturdiness and elaboration in an artwork should be close to identical with the maximum criterion. That is, we view excessive craftsmanship in art as a vulgarity fully as distracting as shoddiness. An artwork should be made exactly and only as well as it must be for its idea to be realized.

Deacon has violated this principle relentlessly. Indeed, a powerful impression of over-the-top craftsmanship is a keynote of his poetic – of the Deaconian. It amounts to an original sculptural diction that is both formally impressive and comical, like an Armani suit on a horse. Elsewhere I have called this quality of Deacon's art 'the tone of labour'. It is a high tone, a toniness, a showy expenditure, and yet innocent of pretension. The labour is of an old-fashioned, artisanal, small-industrial-shop kind, and its motive feels earnest rather than gratuitous. It conveys a certain anxiety, as if afrighted by visions of probably physical ordeals in a world less considerate of art that we assume ours to be.

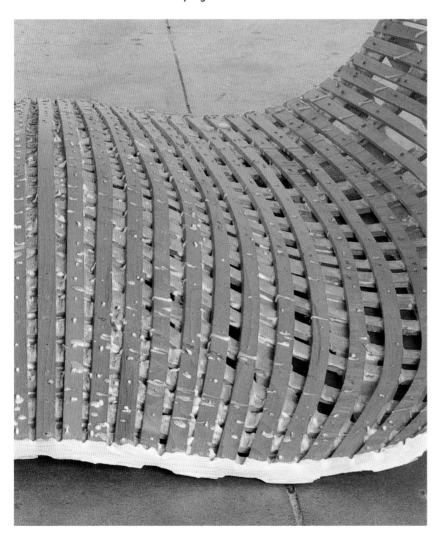

There are hundreds of screw holes. (Where are those proletarian screws today? Have they moved on to serve other projects, or have they joined the reserve army of the unemployed?) There is a profligate amount of glue, bleeding from the joints and buttered around the edges of the two ends (making those edges read as 'lips'). (You know that the sculpture is right-side-up, by the way, by observing the glops and speckles of glue that fell on the interior humped expanse.) And the slats!

They are beautiful forms in themselves, some of the slats that must bend severely in both longitude and latitude to follow the overall contour. If you could hold just one of these in your hands, knowing nothing else about the sculpture, you would have an accurate sense of the strength, precision and grace of the object it was engineered to be part of. Deacon's use of the slats' thin, naked maple celebrates the talent and, when in skilled and respectful hands, the eager obligingness of wood.

There are three layers of slats: forty wide ones running lengthwise outside, a lesser number of somewhat narrower ones hugging the circumference underneath, and about a hundred rib-like ones, narrower still, forming the inner wall. The strength of the crisscross, which gathers into an hourglass-shaped mesh from end to end across the top, is obviously formidable. (Basketry is not evoked, by the way: no interweaving.) Assuming that the glue is sufficiently tenacious, nothing at all should happen if you jump on the sculpture. (Don't, though.)

Keeping the Faith crouches low to the floor, coming up to just above knee level. This disposition feels vaguely aggressive, as if the thing considered biting you in the ankle. But the threat is never imminent. The form looks more aggressive – more whooshy and tigerish – the farther from it you are. It is energized by distance. Up close, as you look down at it, it may suggest a surreally gawky item of furniture, a funhouse coffee table, if it suggests anything. More likely, you will be lost in contemplating details of the construction – like brushstrokes when you step within the inner limit of a painting's pictorial illusion.

So there is a doubleness of aspect: what the form suggests and how the form is put together. Is such doubleness intrinsic to all and any art? Exactly. Its routine emphasis in Deacon's work helps to explain why he is a major artist. He renders dramatically specific in each art object things that are true of art objects generally. He brings to exacerbated consciousness at the same time idiosyncratic feeling and aesthetic phenomena. Major artists are philosophers of art. Deacon is a philosopher of art.

Where would you put Keeping the Faith if you owned it? It would hardly matter so long as the site afforded access to the work in the round. I have seen it in a gallery and in a warehouse. It looked identically fine and awkward in both places – fine because it engaged me in its protocols of meaning and awkward because it felt essentially oblivious to its surroundings, where it seemed less architecturally installed than parked and 'in the way'. I love all of Deacon's work for its reliable independence of the gestalts of institutional space. In any space, it seems to be on my side, to know how I feel, even to be like me: a citizen never quite comfortable in the world.

To commune most frankly with the sculpture, you will squat down as you do when conversing with a small child. At eye-level, the pinched-oval, wailing mouth confides its message in a rush. The message is the package of negative space, of nothingness, inside the two-chambered pod that may seem no longer shaped from without but swelled from within, like lungs or a bellows. The hump in the bottom may suddenly suggest an instrument of speech: a glottis. The glue-lipped mouth forms a syllable that means exactly so much space configured in just this way.

Some religious people speak of emotional emptiness as 'a God-shaped hole'. It is a lovely idea even if you don't believe it: that we contain spiritual cavities into which God fits like a key. I confess to knowing the empty feeling, an inner void – a core of nothing – that, lacking all sensation, can be more awful than pain. I take fleeting comfort in the God-shaped-hole metaphor, which redescribes the emptiness from an affliction to a capacity.

I am pretty sure of going beyond, in this, what Deacon had in mind for his sculpture, if indeed he had something in mind. Not 'to have in mind', passively, but 'to mind', actively, is what a good artist does, making through selfless concentration on the actual work an unprejudiced medium for the expression of whatever is there to be expressed in the artist's or viewer's unconscious, or in the air. But by choosing for his title the phrase 'keeping the faith', Deacon indicates that he notices something about his idea, and the associative process thus begun emboldens my interpretation.

In vernacular use, 'keep the faith' is an injunction to stay loyal to a value or a cause. It was popularized in the 1960s by an old-time Harlem politician, Adam Clayton Powell Jr., whose insolently loose morals, outraging the middle class, targeted him for destruction in government circles and the press. 'Keep the faith, baby', he would say, appealing to a constituency meant to understand his essential oneness with them beneath corrupt appearances. Powell's 'faith' was an invisible integrity.

So is any faith, defined as confidence in the reality of something rationally unprovable. *Keeping the Faith*, the sculpture, goes to tremendous trouble to form and to preserve – to keep – a strangely shaped quantity of air. The effort symbolizes the importance of keeping. Faith is not symbolized. It is a fact or it isn't, understood or not understood, meaningful or nonsensical. Its proposition does not brook argument. What you get from the sculpture is the sheer, mere urgency of something unseen. What your heart does with that is your heart's affair.

overleaf, Installation, Marian Goodman Gallery, New York
1992
l. to r., **Substance, The Interior Is Always More Difficult (J), In the Flesh, Keeping the Faith,** all works, 1992

Contents

Interview Pier Luigi Tazzi in conversation with Richard Deacon, page 6. **Survey** Jon Thompson

Thinking Richard Deacon, Thinking Sculptor, Thinking Sculpture, page 36. **Focus** Peter Schjeldahl Deacon's Faith,

page 88. **Artist's Choice** Mary Douglas Purity and Danger, 1966, **page 98.** **Artist's**

Writings Richard Deacon Selections from Stuff Box Object, 1971-72, **page 110.** Artist's Statement, 1982, page 114.

Silence, Exile, Cunning, 1986-88, **page 116.** What Car? Correspondence with Lynne Cooke, 1992 **page 120.** What You See Is What

You Get, 1992, **page 132.** Design for Replacing, 1987, **page 138.** Design for Factory, 1993, **page 139.** Reading: a propos de Toni

Grand, 1993, page 140. **Chronology** page 144 & Bibliography, page 158.

Now to confront our opening question. Can there be any people who confound sacredness with uncleanness? We have seen how the idea of contagion is at work in religion and society. We have seen that powers are attributed to any structure of ideas, and that rules of avoidance make a visible public recognition of its boundaries. But this is not to say that the sacred is unclean. Each culture must have its own notions of dirt and defilement which are contrasted with its notions of the positive structure which must not be negated. To talk about a confused blending of the Sacred and the Unclean is outright nonsense. But it still remains true that religions often sacralize the very unclean things which have been rejected with abhorrence. We must, therefore, ask how dirt, which is normally destructive, sometimes becomes creative.

First, we note that not all unclean things are used constructively in ritual. It does not suffice for something to be unclean for it to be treated as potent for good. In Israel it was unthinkable that unclean things, such as corpses and excreta, could be incorporated into the Temple ritual, but only blood, and only blood shed in sacrifice. Among the Oyo Yoruba where the left hand is used for unclean work and it is deeply insulting to proffer the left hand, normal rituals sacralize the precedence of the right side, especially dancing to the right. But in the ritual of the great Ogboni cult initiates must knot their garments on the left side and dance only to the left (Morton-Williams, p. 369). Incest is a pollution among the Bushong, but an act of ritual incest is part of the sacralization of their king and he claims that he is the filth of the nation: '*Moi, ordure, nyec*' (Vansina, p. 103). And so on. Though it is only specific individuals on specified occasions who can break the rules, it is still important to ask why these dangerous contacts are often required in rituals.

If the Shoe Fits
1981
Galvanized corrugated sheet
steel, screws
152 × 331 × 152 cm

Boys and Girls
1982
Linoleum, plywood
91.5 × 183 × 152.5 cm
Collection, The British Council,
London

One answer lies in the nature of dirt itself. The other lies in the nature of metaphysical problems and of particular kinds of reflections which call for expression.

To deal with dirt first. In the course of any imposing of order, whether in the mind or in the external world, the attitude to rejected bits and pieces goes through two stages. First they are recognizably out of place, a threat to good order, and so are regarded as objectionable and vigorously brushed away. At this stage they have some identity: they can be seen to be unwanted bits of whatever it was they came from, hair or food or wrappings. This is the stage at which they are dangerous; their half-identity still clings to them and the clarity of the scene in which they obtrude is impaired by their presence. But a long process of pulverizing, dissolving and rotting awaits any physical things that have been recognized as dirt. In the end, all identity is gone. The origin of the various bits and pieces is lost and they have entered into the mass of common rubbish. It is unpleasant to poke about in the refuse to try to recover anything, for this revives identity. So long as identity is absent, rubbish is not dangerous. It does not even create ambiguous perceptions since it clearly belongs in a defined place, a rubbish heap of one kind or another. Even the bones of buried kings rouse little awe and the thought that the air is full of the dust of corpses of bygone races has no power to move. Where there is no differentiation there is no defilement.

> They outnumber the living, but where are all their bones?
> For every man alive there are a million dead,
> Has their dust gone into earth that it is never seen?
> There should be no air to breathe, with it so thick,
> No space for wind to blow or rain to fall:
> Earth should be a cloud of dust, a soil of bones,
> With no room even for our skeletons.
> It is wasted time to think of it, to count its grains.
> When all are alike and there is no difference in them.

S. Sitwell, *Agamemnon's Tomb*

In this final stage of total disintegration, dirt is utterly undifferentiated. Thus a cycle has been completed. Dirt was created by the differentiating activity of mind, it was a by-product of the creation of order. So it started from a state of non-differentiation; all through the process of differentiating its role was to threaten the distinctions made; finally it returns to its true indiscriminable character. Formlessness is therefore an apt symbol of beginning and of growth as it is of decay.

On this argument everything that is said to explain the revivifying role of water in religious symbolism can also apply to dirt:

> In water everything is 'dissolved', every 'form' is broken up, everything that has happened ceases to exist; nothing that was before remains after immersion in water, not an outline, not a 'sign', not an event. Immersion is the equivalent, at the human level, of death at the cosmic level, of the cataclysm (the Flood) which periodically dissolves the world into the primeval ocean. Breaking up all forms, doing away with the past, water possesses this power of purifying, of regenerating, of giving new birth … Water purifies and regenerates because it nullifies the past, and restores – even if only for a moment – the integrity of the dawn of things

Eliade, 1958, p. 194

The Back of My Hand No 1
1986
Galvanized steel, linoleum
366 × 244 × 46 cm
Installation, Interim Art, London

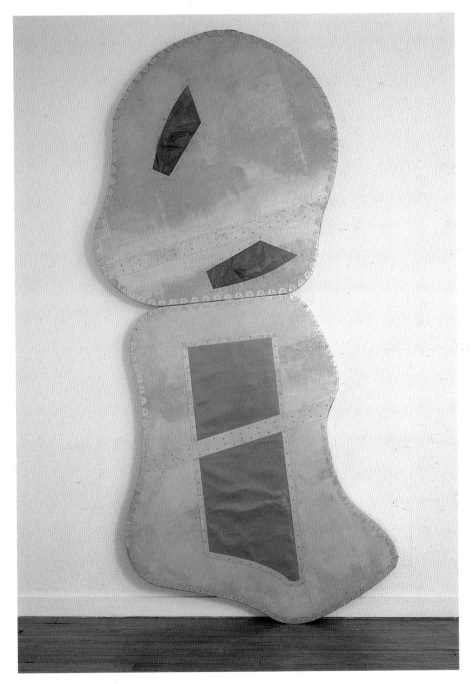

The Back of My Hand No 4
1986
Galvanized steel, leather, PVC
sheet
280 × 150 × 20 cm
Collection, Centre Georges
Pompidou, Paris

In the same book Eliade goes on to assimilate with water two other symbols of renewal which we can, without labouring the point, equally associate with dust and corruption. One is symbolism of darkness and the other orgiastic celebration of the New Year (pp. 398-9).

In its last phase then, dirt shows itself as an apt symbol of creative formlessness. But it is from its first phase that it derives its force. The danger which is risked by boundary transgression is power. Those vulnerable margins and those attacking forces which threaten to destroy good order represent the powers inhering in the cosmos. Ritual which can harness these for good is harnessing power indeed.

So much for the aptness of the symbol itself. Now for the living situations to which it applies, and which are irremediably subject to paradox. The quest for purity is pursued by rejection. It follows that when purity is not a symbol but something lived, it must be poor and barren. It is part of our condition that the purity for which we strive and sacrifice so much turns out to be hard and dead as a stone when we get it. It is all very well for the poet to praise winter as the

Paragon of art,
That kills all forms of life and feeling
Save what is pure and will survive.

Roy Campbell

It is another thing to try and make over our existence into an unchanging lapidary form. Purity is the enemy of change, of ambiguity and compromise. Most of us indeed would feel safer if our existence could be hard-set and fixed in form. As Sartre wrote so bitterly of the anti-semite:

How can anyone choose to reason falsely? It is simply the old yearning for impermeability … there are people who are attracted by the permanence of stone. They would like to be solid and impenetrable, they do not want change: for who knows what change might bring? … It is as if their own existence were perpetually in suspense. But they want to exist in all ways at once, and all in one instant. They have no wish to acquire ideas, they want them to be innate … they want to adopt a mode of life in which reasoning and the quest for truth play only a subordinate part, in which nothing is sought except what has already been found, in which one never becomes anything else but what one already was. (1948)

This diatribe implies a division between ours and the rigid black and white thinking of the anti-semite. Whereas, of course, the yearning for rigidity is in us all. It is part of our human condition to long for hard lines and clear concepts. When we have them we have to either face the fact that some realities elude them, or else blind ourselves to the inadequacy of the concepts.

The final paradox of the search for purity is that it is an attempt to force experience into logical categories of non-contradiction. But experience is not amenable and those who make the attempt find themselves led into contradiction.

Where sexual purity is concerned it is obvious that if it is to imply no contact between the sexes it is not only a denial of sex, but must be literally barren. It also leads to contradiction. To wish all women to be chaste at all times goes contrary to other wishes and if followed consistently leads to inconveniences of the kind to which Mae Enga men submit. High-born girls of 17th century Spain found themselves in a dilemma in which dishonour stood on either horn. St. Theresa of Avila was brought up in a society in which the seduction of a girl had to be avenged by her brother or father. So if she received a lover she risked dishonour and the lives of men. But her personal honour required her to be generous and not to withhold herself from her lover, as it was unthinkable to shun lovers altogether. There are many other examples of how the quest for purity creates problems and some curious solutions.

One solution is to enjoy purity at second hand. Something of a vicarious satisfaction gave its aura, no doubt, to the respect for virginity in early Christendom, gives extra zest to the Nambudiri Brahmins when they enclose their sisters, and enhances the prestige of Brahmins among lower castes in general. In certain chiefdoms the Pende of the Kasai expect their chiefs to live in sexual continence. Thus one man conserves the wellbeing of the chiefdom on behalf of his polygamous subjects. To ensure no lapse on the part of the chief, who is admittedly past his prime when installed, his subjects fix a penis sheath on him for life (de Sousberghe).

left, **Art for Other People No 26**
1987-88
Galvanized steel, PVC, butyl
rubber, canvas
10 × 62 × 62 cm

right, **Art for Other People No 28**
1990
Steel, foam, polyester resin
2 parts, 15.2 × 76.2 × 61 cm each

Sometimes the claim to superior purity is based on deceit. The adult men of the Chagga tribe used to pretend that at initiation their anus was blocked for life. Initiated men were supposed never to need to defecate, unlike women and children who remained subject to the exigency of their bodies (Raum). Imagine the complications into which this pretence led Chagga men. The moral of all this is that the facts of existence are a chaotic jumble. If we select from the body's image a few aspects which do not offend, we must be prepared to suffer for the distortion. The body is not a lightly porous jug. To switch the metaphor, a garden is not a tapestry; if all the weeds are removed, the soil is impoverished. Somehow the gardener must preserve fertility by returning what he has taken out. The special kind of treatment which some religions accord to anomalies and abominations to make them powerful for good is like turning weeds and lawn cuttings into compost.

This is the general outline for an answer to why pollutions are often used in renewal rites.

Whenever a strict pattern of purity is imposed on our lives it is either highly uncomfortable or it leads into contradiction if closely followed, or it leads to hypocrisy. That which is negated is not thereby removed. The rest of life, which does not tidily fit the accepted categories, is still there and demands attention. The body, as we have tried to show, provides a basic scheme for all symbolism. There is hardly any pollution which does not have some primary physiological reference. As life is in the body it cannot be rejected outright. And as life must be affirmed, the most complete philosophies, as William James put it, must find some ultimate way of affirming that which has been rejected.

If we admit that evil is an essential part of our being and the key to the interpretation of our life, we load ourselves down with a difficulty that has always proved burdensome in philosophies of religion. Theism, wherever it has erected itself into a systematic philosophy of the universe, has shown a reluctance to let God be anything less than All-in-All ... at variance with popular theism (is a philosophy) which is frankly pluralistic ... the universe compounded of many original principles ... God is not necessarily responsible for the existence of evil. The gospel of healthy-mindedness casts its vote distinctly for this pluralistic view. Whereas the monistic philosopher finds himself more or less bound to say, as Hegel said, that everything actual is rational, and that evil, as an element dialectically required, must be pinned in, and kept and consecrated and have a function awarded to it in the final system of truth, healthy-mindedness refuses to say anything of the sort. Evil, it says, is emphatically irrational, and not to be pinned in, or preserved or consecrated in any final system of truth. It is a pure abomination to the Lord, an alien unreality, a waste element, to be sloughed off and negated ... the ideal, so far from being co-extensive with the actual, is a mere extract from the actual, marked by its deliverance from all contact with this diseased, inferior, excrementitious stuff.

Here we have the interesting notion ... of there being elements of the universe which may make no rational whole in conjunction with the other elements, and which, from the point of view of any system which those elements make up, can only be considered so much irrelevance and accident – so much 'dirt' as it were, and matter out of place. (p.129)

Out of the House
1983
Galvanized steel, rivets, linoleum
122 × 61 × 152.5 cm

Artist's Choice

BUTTER
OIL
VINEGAR
WASHING POWDER
SHALLOTS
PASTA
SALAD STUFF
(TONIGHT) BBQ

Contents

Interview Pier Luigi Tazzi in conversation with Richard Deacon, page 6. Survey Jon Thompson Thinking Richard Deacon, Thinking Sculptor, Thinking Sculpture, page 36. Focus Peter Schjeldahl Deacon's Faith, page 88. Artist's Choice Mary Douglas Purity and Danger, 1966, page 98. Artist's Writings Richard Deacon Selections from Stuff Box Object, 1971-72, page 110. Artist's Statement, 1982, page 114. Silence, Exile, Cunning, 1986-88, page 116. What Car? Correspondence with Lynne Cooke, 1992 page 120. What You See Is What You Get, 1992, page 132. Design for Replacing, 1987, page 138. Design for Factory, 1993, page 139. Reading: a propos de Toni Grand, 1993, page 140. Chronology page 144 & Bibliography, page 158.

Stuff Box Object
1970-71

I shovelled the Stuff into the wall half of the area, creating a bank eight feet long, two wide and one high and fixed a plank along the front to prevent it spreading.

When the Stuff was soft and well mixed I built a container around and over it – three feet high by eight by two – made of old floorboards nailed vertically onto a frame of thick planks.

I held the pounder handle in both hands, lifted it high and drove it down on top of the Stuff, walking around from place to place inside the container.

I took to pieces the container surrounding the Stuff, which remained in a solid block. I removed all of the nails from the wood and stacked it with the two tools. A mouse ran out.

On that evening Ted suggested that he and I exchange locations and materials, each of us leaving things as they were and proceeding to the other's location. I agreed to the exchange. I undertook a responsibility towards the condition of the Stuff that I placed in the exchange. In handing it over to Ted I expected him to attend to its care. My responsibility was extended towards the things that I received from the exchange. I received a large wooden Box, an amount of raw Flax joined by strips of Fibre Glass, Straw, Chicken Shit and scraps of Wood. The Box dominated the exchange. Its base was two and a half by three feet. It stood just over three feet high. Into the top, which was not attached and could be lifted, were screwed two large Butt-Hinges and two long Bolts. The inside of the Box was coated with Lard, which had soaked in and was starting to rot the Wood. The Box smelt rancid.

On Monday January 19 I began to prepare the Box. In the centre of each side and in the top I drilled five holes, one hole in the dead centre and the other four forming a square around it – the pattern used to indicate a five on a die. I mounted a light inside the top, the flex going out to a socket through the central hole. I set a bolt inside the top, screwed two hasps onto the outside and padlocked the Box shut.

On the morning of Friday January 23, watched by Peter Atkins and Robert Bell and wearing a White Boiler Suit, I unlocked the Box and opened the top. I placed inside a knife, a hammer, a bag of tacks, a roll of carpet and a clock. I turned on the light and climbed inside, closing and bolting the top behind me.

Inside, I adopted a foetal position on first closing the top; body curled, head bent over, legs together, knees drawn up against my chest. In this position I fitted my body across the Box between diagonally opposed corners. I turned over. It was only possible to turn from side to side and not to do a full turn – either by going head-over-heels or by rolling lengthwise. By pushing parts of my body against the sides while relaxing and moving others I moved around the Box. It was hot and greasy inside and I started to

Stuff Box Object
1970-71

Stuff Box Object
1970-71

sweat heavily. Turning from one side to the other I became careless and my left leg smashed the light bulb in the top. I slid the bolt back, opened the top, climbed out, shut and padlocked the Box and left.

18/5/71; 10:20. I change into the Boiler Suit, fetch an old sheet of hardboard and lay it on the floor beside the Object. I fill a bucket with sand, carry it across and tip it out on the hardboard. From the bag of cement standing next to the bag of sand I measure out half a bucket, carry it across to the hardboard and tip the cement into the sand. I turn the two together with a spade and fetch water in two buckets, a pint in one and the other full. I tip a pint of Uni-Bond (bonding adhesive) into the first and use the water from the other bucket to wet the cement. When the cement is ready I improvise a board and trowel some cement onto it. Resting the board against the Object and being careful that the cement does not slip to the floor, I pick up a paint brush and the bucket of bond and paint one edge of the Object. I place the bucket on the floor, stand the paint brush in it, pick up the trowel and the loaded board and cement the wet edge, squaring and levelling the corner. I finish, place the board and trowel down on top of the Object, pick up the bucket and brush and paint a second edge with bond. I place the bucket on the floor, cut out a piece of sacking, wet it and lay it over the first edge. I trowel more cement onto the Board and commence squaring and levelling the second edge. I continue until all the edges are done. I inspect the whole surface of the Object, painting over faults in the cement with bond and filling them. I cover the Object completely with damp sacking and clean up – scrape the floor free of excess cement, push the waste into a pile then throw it into a dustbin, take the piece of hardboard off the floor and stack it against a wall, wash the trowel, the board and the spade free of cement and put them away. I wash out the paint brush and cover the bucket of bond, remove the Boiler Suit and wash my hands.

3:45. I remove the covers and nail a skirting board around the bottom of the Object. As I nail several large pieces of cement fall off the corners. At 6:00 I replace the covers on the object, clean up the floor and leave the Studio.

19/5/71; 11:30. I change into the Boiler Suit, take up what remains of the bond, uncover the Object and paint over the damaged sections of the cement. I lay the piece of hardboard out on the floor next to the Object, tip a bucketful of sand and half of cement onto it and mix the two together. When the dry mix is ready I wet it. I take up the trowel and board and use the trowel to scrape the board free of dry cement. I trowel some cement onto the board and commence repairing the damage. After finishing there is cement left, so I paint bond onto the sides of the object shown by the skirting board to be irregular and finish off the cement by building up depressed areas. I finish at 1:10,

Stuff Box Object
1970-71

clean around the Object, stack the hardboard up, wash the trowel and the spade free of cement, remove the Boiler Suit, wash my hands and go to lunch.

20/5/71; 2:10. I scrape down the surface of the Object, removing any flakes of cement and preparing the surface for plastering. I make a board to hold plaster and paint one side of the Object with bond. I put on the Boiler Suit, open a bag of siraptite plaster and mix up wet plaster in a bowl. I fetch the trowel and start plastering the painted end of the Object. I find the plaster sticky and stiff to the trowel, harder to work than cement. I have almost finished the side when Ted comes up and tells me how to do it. He says that I am laying the plaster on too thick, that I should be quick with the trowel, moving it rapidly across the surface being plastered and that I should keep the plaster surface very wet so that I can move it around with ease. I give him the trowel and he shows me how, indicating the direction of stroke with the trowel and the right wetness and thickness of plaster to be using. I watch everything that Ted does. At 3:45 we run out of plaster. I wash the trowel, the board and the bowl and remove the Boiler Suit. We go to tea.

21/5/71; 10:15. I put on the Boiler Suit, fetch some water in the bowl, pick up a bag of plaster and sprinkle some into the water in the bowl, mixing it up. I take up the trowel and the board, wet them both and trowel some plaster onto the board. I wet one of the two unplastered sides of the Object and start plastering. I work upwards and outwards from the middle of the side at the bottom, where the cement level is depressed. I use the plaster wetter and lay it down thinner and faster than previously. I finish the mixed plaster and buy some more, mix up a fresh batch, wet the final side and commence plastering, again working upwards and outwards from the centre at the bottom. I finish and examine the Object. The side that Ted and I plastered between us is fully covered, but the finish is bad and needs cleaning up. The other three sides are much neater but each needs more plaster to level and cover it. I wash the trowel, the board and the bowl, remove the Boiler Suit and wash my hands. Using a cold chisel I start scraping down and tidying the first side plastered. I stop after a short time and decide to wait until the plastering is finished before continuing.

21/6/71; 9:45. I change into the Boiler Suit, remove my shoes and step into a pair of boots. I take up the bucket and remove from it the hammer and chisel, the trowel, the paint brush, a ball of string and a nail tied to a short piece of string, placing them all on the floor. I fill the bucket with water, pour some into the bowl and place the bucket on the floor beside the Object. I place the bowl beside the sack of plaster, take plaster from the sack and sprinkle it into the water in the bowl, mixing the two together. I carry the bowl of wet plaster to the end of the Object furthest from the door and face it, holding the

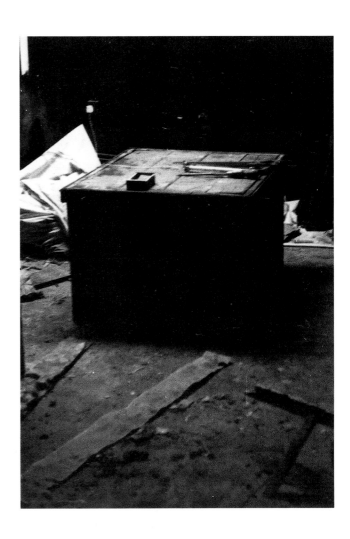

Stuff Box Object
1970-71

bowl in my left hand. I tilt the bowl away from me, plunge my right hand into the plaster and flick it out towards the Object, transferring plaster to the surface. I flick from the left to right across the top, drop the bowl and my hand about six inches and flick from the right to left back. I continue working back and forth across the surface until the bowl is empty. I wash my right hand in the water in the bucket, tip water into the bowl, rinse it around and leave the bowl on the floor. I pick up a length of wood and, holding it horizontally, stand facing the plastered end of the Object. I bend my knees and apply the wood across the runners at the bottom. I straighten my legs and run the wood up along the runners, keeping it pressed hard against them. Fresh plaster projecting beyond the plane of the runners is scraped off and builds up on the wood. I pick the plaster off the wood and stuff it into holes in the plaster surface. When the wood ceases to gather plaster on its run, I rest it against the Object, wash the bowl and my hands and empty the bucket. I place the bowl and the bucket down on the floor, the bucket inside the bowl, remove the Boiler Suit and hang it up, change my boots for my shoes.

22/6/71; 2:05. I fetch a rasp from the sculpture department stores and use it on the two 'flicked' ends of the Object. The plaster has built up dry on both of these beyond the level set by the runners and the wood is forced away and ceases to establish a true surface in use. I use the rasp for five minutes, working on the end of the Object nearest the door, place it on top and fetch the hammer and chisel from the floor at the opposite end. I chisel down the plaster, working from top to bottom and checking the level by looking across the runners. I get the level right for the top six to nine inches, place the hammer and chisel on top of the Object and pick up the rasp to smooth the surface. I work on the end for half an hour, finally check the level by running a piece of wood between the runners, place the rasp beside the hammer and chisel and leave the Studio.

St. Martin's School of Art, London, 1971-72. Re-edited and published by the Chapter Arts Centre, Cardiff, 1984

Stuff Box Object
1970-71

Artist's Statement 1982

Jacqui (Poncelet) and I moved to Brixton in April 1976. In November of the same year Acme was provisionally granted a lease on the factory at 52 Acre Lane and work began on making the building watertight, restoring services and dividing up the studios. By February 1977 I was using my studio. In January 1978 my son was born. That September we went to the United States for a year, returning to the same house and the same studio. In August 1978 and again in June 1980 I used the gallery which has become incorporated into the Acre Lane studios to show my work.

These seem to me to be important facts of my life over the past six years. I don't know what relation the work I have done has to them. There are certain things – the light and space in my studio are important to me, it is a place that I enjoy going to; a great deal of the material that I have used has been scrap salvaged from the conversion of the factory, collected and stored; the gallery at the studios is a liberating facility. And there are people – I have felt a strong sense of community with the individual artists who occupy the studio at Acre Lane, particularly at the beginning when we were all trying to make the building work and trying to make studios for ourselves; Peter Venn, who had the studio next to mine before he moved to Norfolk, and Bill Woodrow who lives near and also has a studio at Acre Lane are both old friends with whom, in different ways, I feel a strong kinship; Matt Rugg whom I met through the studios is another; I could go on to talk about neighbours and friends who live nearby. More intangibly South London in general and Brixton in particular seems to me to be a very open place, I have found the opportunity to do what, at an individual level, matters very much and to find support for doing it. I have come to feel that I belong here.

There are also the crushing realities of urban decay, economic deprivation, unemployment and racism. In the face of these facts I am less optimistic, less sure.

'The South Bank Show' (cat.), South Bank Centre, London, 1982

Only the Lonely, exhibition with
Bill Woodrow, Chisenhale Gallery,
London, 1993
l. to r., **Wooly Bully**, 1993;
Only the Lonely, 1993;
Democratic Process, 1990;
Night and Day, 1992;
Thought It Was a Duck, 1992;
Whatcha Goin' to Do About It,
1993;
Doin' the Do, 1992

Silence, Exile, Cunning (extract) 1986-88

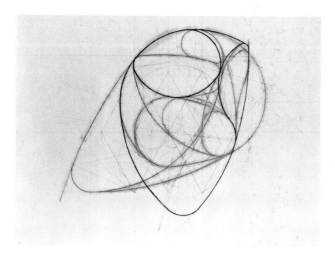

**It's Orpheus When There's
Singing No 7**
1979
Oil pastel, graphite on paper
112 × 147.5 cm
Collection, Weltkunst Foundation,
Zurich

In December 1978 I went to the United States for a year. I left London with a happy feeling in my heart and a sense of optimism. Up until that point, I had done a certain number of things, but was still feeling dissatisfied by what I had accomplished. Going somewhere else seemed to offer a situation where familiarity, habit and expectation could be left behind, and I could become what I wanted to be. Going was as much leaving as arriving. In the States I would be faced with deciding what to do.

For some years previously I'd been reading Rilke, mainly his letters and his essay on Rodin. In New York, and indeed on the plane to New York, I began to read his *Sonnets to Orpheus*. I read them time and time again over the next five months. I began to make drawings, and at some point it became apparent that what I was drawing had a very distinct relationship to what I was reading. But elucidating exactly what the relationship was is more difficult.

The first thing that attracted me to the *Sonnets*, I remember, was the way in which Rilke wrote of speech and, particularly, of song and of praise. Song and praise here are *US* and, at the same time, that which shapes the world:

> *song is existence. For the god unstrained*
> *But when shall we exist? ...*

The elements of the Orphic myth – the singer whose song can charm the beasts, cause the rocks and the trees to move, and draw Eurydice back from the dead; and whose body is torn apart and scattered by the Maenads, his head floating off still singing – provide a peg on which these reciprocating ideas can be hung.

> *Raise no commemorating store. The roses*
> *shall blossom every summer for his sake.*
> *For this is Orpheus. His metamorphosis*
> *is this one and that. We should not make*
> *searches for other names. Once and for all,*
> *it's Orpheus when there's song. He comes*
> *   and goes.*
> *Is it not much if sometimes, by some small*
> *number of days, he shall outlive the rose.*

To sing or to praise not only describes the world but brings it into being – as if to say the right name by some resonance shapes the stuff of the world into this or that thing – or at least allows the particular thing to be distinguished. If this is so, then language – the place where speaking occurs – is itself our world.

At the same time, there is no speaking without listening, hearing is a part of singing.

Untitled
1980
Galvanized steel, concrete
125 × 345 × 125 cm

We are both listeners and speakers; we are of and in language.

Though they destroyed you at last and
  revenge had its will,
sound of you lingered in lions and rocks
  you were first to
enthral, in the trees and birds. You are
  singing there still.

O you god that has vanished. You infinite
  track.
Only because dismembering hatred
  dispersed you
are we hearers today and a mouth which
  else Nature would lack.

Reciprocity and reflexivity are at the heart of the drawings, which are by no means literal representations of aspects of the poems. The entire suite is collectively titled *It's Orpheus When There's Singing*. All the drawings have an enclosure, an enclosing line, with, at some point, an aperture circumscribed by the enclosure. The aperture and the whole enclosure can be thought of as the head of Orpheus. In the world there are a large number of items you come across frequently – shoes, hats, pots, pans, cups, jugs, shells, bags, pockets, gloves, etc. – which have a similar form – an enclosure with a small opening. Rather than being straightforward images of a head, the drawings referred to the other things, sometimes very obviously.

There are also the questions of what an enclosure is, and what an opening is. An enclosure is a formation, a clarification, actuality; an opening is a possibility. Singing and listening are reciprocal activities. Mouths and ears are openings in the head. Both seem to imply resonance: sound comes out of and goes into hollowness. The dog on the His Master's Voice recording label can listen *and* bark.

There was no object being drawn, so in order to get to a point where I could draw what I wanted, it seemed necessary to have rules. These were a means of avoiding some decisions about the appearance of the drawing as it developed. The drawings were constructed using a string, a pin and a pencil – this was the rule. All the curves were then built up from arcs or segments of circles of varying radii. This construction created a very fine mesh of marks, from which a final form slowly emerged, almost as if it had been captured.

Artist's Writings

Untitled
1981
Laminated wood
140 × 305 × 216 cm
Collection, Fonds National d'Art
Contemporain, Paris

While the first drawings were concerned with a parallel between an enclosure and a human head, the later ones were concerned with aspects of picturing, recognition and identification implicit in the line being constructed. I think that a part of the fruitfulness of these drawings in respect to other work has to do with their method of being built: they are not pictures or plans, but rather constitute something like a grammar. Somehow, they were 'in anticipation'.

Since speech is constitutive of ourselves as human, to speak is both to cause the world to be and to be oneself. At the same time, speech is not a thing, but rather a product of community, built bit by bit in discourse. Speech is not nature, like stone or rock; it is manufactured. To make is also to bring into being, to cause there to be something.

When I returned to England, I had these drawings in mind as being potentially important for the sculpture that I might make. Of course, making a drawing is different from making a sculpture. The drawings seemed to show that what was enclosed had a relationship to the contour. This functioned like a skin over the interior, and the interior remained a hollow resonant space. But both 'skin' and 'interior' remain separate and mute, though the elements of language, appearance, community, building, speaking, listening, production and manufacture all seem to be involved.

> *A tree ascending there. O pure transcension.*
> *O Orpheus sings. O tall tree in the ear.*
> *All else is suspended, yet in that suspension*
> *what new beginning, beckoning, change appear.*
>
> *Creatures of silence pressing through the clear*
> *disintricated wood from lair and nest;*
> *and neither cunning, it grew manifest,*
> *had made them breathe so quietly, nor fear,*
>
> *But only hearing. Roar, cry, bell they found*
> *within their hearts too small. And where before*
> *less than a hurt had harboured what came thronging,*
>
> *a refuge tunnelled out of dimmest longing*
> *with lowly entrance through a quivering door,*
> *you build temples in their sense of sound.*

'Richard Deacon' (cat.), Carnegie Museum of Art, Pittsburgh, 1988

Richard Deacon, 20 February, 1992

A car stands in front of a glazed, bland but convoluted building. A pared down, corporate, late modernist exterior. Surrounding buildings are amongst the welter of reflections and self-reflections in the glass. The glazing pattern of the building is in turn reflected in the car windscreen. The plaza is stepped, the paving detailed with stripes. A fragment, an inverted 'V' shape, is visible to one side behind the car. This is possibly a sculptural, possibly a structural element. Behind this a piece of movable security fencing has been placed across a (side?) doorway. Another doorway is visible to the rear of the image, again closed and visually obstructed by the stepped detailing of the plaza. These are the only visible entrances to the building, both closed. Within the car's interior it is possible to make out the four seat headrests and to know that there is no-one inside. The driver's door is presented to the spectator, the prominent side mirror at the very centre of the image. Reflections in the windscreen marry car and building; to be inside the one is to be inside the other; to be outside is to be outside them both. The car seems to occupy a place in a corporate plaza that, most frequently in North America, Japan or Germany, would be taken by an artwork. The copy says 'The Chairman's Statement', a nice conjunction of the form of address within a shareholders meeting with, given the clues from the rest of the image, the idea of artistic utterance. The corporate high flyer is joined to the personalized and individualistic values associated with the artist and artwork. The raising of a vehicle to iconic or symbolic status should come as no surprise yet the device by which that is accomplished in this particular case is worth marking. The plaza, even a corporate one, is a public place. Sculpture has been used to both adorn that space and to celebrate its publicness. Although as Richard Serra has discovered there are limits, freedom of expression belongs in the public domain. There is also a sense in which the implicit act of patronage is celebrated.

There are no people in the picture and half of the population are non participators.

Lynne Cooke, 14 March, 1992

This pristine, newly-minted car astride the corporate plaza usurps, as you say, Richard, the place that would, if occupied, normally be taken by an art-object. What makes the substitution so provocative is, it seems to me, the way that the vehicle usurps the place but not necessarily the role of the artwork; indeed it seems actively to embrace that very role. To the degree that it succeeds it becomes an interlocutor not an impostor.

Much twentieth century sculpture in the public domain, which increasingly means the corporate as much as state or municipal environs, simply adorns its environment. Seeking to

Between the Eyes
1990
Mild painted steel, stainless steel,
cement, granite base
800 × 1900 × 700 cm
Yonge Square, Toronto

ameliorate the visual cacophony of street signs and 'furniture' that make up the urban space, to embellish or otherwise provide a respite from this clamour, only rarely does the sculpture escape being commandeered as a logo, a sign naming the site in shorthand. Seldom does it manage to offer a counterstatement or even an explicit commentary on the values enshrined in that locale, as Richard Serra's *Tilted Arc* so effectively, if provocatively, did (...)

The functions assumed by the car are thus virtually equivalent, albeit pervertedly so, to those traditionally accorded the monument: to educate, elevate and decorate (in that order). The monument is usually realized in the form of a statue of a heroic figure who is commemorated, even celebrated, for the exemplary character of his (or her) actions, and therefore as a source of moral authority and as a model for civic virtue (or valour). Ironically, and this is something that has not escaped the attention of the advertisers, in contemporary urban society the chairman of the corporation has assumed, even at times seized, such a role. That the values that he (not she, as the image makes only too apparent) embodies revolve around money, power, exclusivity, surface style, mobility and transience, that they are essentially private, and that their sphere and manner of operation is being celebrated here is the message disseminated by the image. That responsibility for this in part lies, as Richard Sennett has persuasively argued, in the fall of public man, that is, in the withering away of the civic roles formerly adopted by the citizen, is a conclusion hard to escape. Similarly, the deduction that public space is merely a fiction, that it has long been occupied by private interests, is one that is hard to deny (...)

Richard Serra
Tilted Arc
1981
Cor-ten steel
345.6 × 3,456 cm

Richard Deacon, 17 March, 1992

The car is not parked, it is there deliberately; the driver has not strode inside for a meeting. It is important that we (those of us whose gender allows this little fantasy) realize this, that availability (ownership?) is a possibility, though vicarious. However it is also true that this is an artifice, the public space exists in this case through a piece of image making. You are also right to expand your frame of reference to take in the whole photograph. I hadn't remarked the poignancy of 'Bush Road' over the rubbish bags but I had noticed the piles of garbage, the graffiti, the brutality of the rendered gable end and that this was an occupied place. Did you ever read a book that came out sometime around 1986, a study of territory in housing estates, particularly the blocks from the sixties with their public walkways, communal areas, etc.? I'll have to try and find the title. The argument was that lack of definition of those communal areas was a strong contributing factor to social breakdown in the blocks. Paradoxically, the best of intentions, by confusing public and private, had engendered alienation and social

confusion, the very symptoms that the architects and the local authorities were trying to alleviate. Against these blocks were contrasted suburban developments of the interwar years, rows of individual houses where the distinction between public and private is absolutely clear. And where, furthermore, baywindows at the front gave an occupier a means of surveillance. The zones of responsibility for maintenance etc. being clearly established, anti-social behaviour is suppressed. The book was quite successful, its recommendations becoming quite influential. The redefinition of occupied space by removal of walkways, addition of gates, abolition of communal areas is being actively pursued by many local authorities. While hopefully this ameliorates the quality of life for residents, it does so by eliminating one sort of public space – the networks of alleys, walkways, stairs and open spaces to which all had access and none had charge. There is an intriguing paradox in the photograph we are considering in that the billboard proposes (suggests) a public space, recognizable as such – the message relies on that recognition – at the same time the photograph itself shows the absence of conditions in which such publicness could endure.

Lynne Cooke, 21 March, 1992
(...) So, fortuitously perhaps but nonetheless tellingly, your photograph counterpoints an image of an uninhabited pristine public space containing a brand new luxury car with actuality, with, that is, a populated mundane street corner at which is parked a utility vehicle, an ordinary commercial van. Both of these are clearly urban sites; the former (supposedly) recently constructed, the latter an unplanned aggregate that has accumulated over time. If one is therefore the paradigmatic architecturally designed location, the other might be characterized as an adventitiously formed fragment of the built environment: where one is seamless, ordered and cohesive the other betrays the ruptures, oppositions and asynchronicity, the margins and transitions that in fact make up the totality of most urban environments.

In certain respects these antithetical sites could be read as two models for the kinds of public spaces currently made available for public sculpture. In neither instance is it easy to recognize that social spaces like these are indeed collectively constructed. Nor can it be easy for the contemporary sculptor to acknowledge, define and perhaps manifest in his or her work, the complexity of the social experience inherent in, or integral to, any such space.

Richard Deacon, 26 March, 1992
'Look at this,' Joe said. In the living room, he sat on the bed, his small suitcase beside

Distance No Object
1988
Painted steel, copper
282 × 579 × 381 cm
Collection, San Francisco Museum
of Modern Art

him; he had opened it and brought out a ragged, bent book which showed signs of much
handling. He grinned at Juliana. 'Come here. You know what somebody says? This man'.
He indicated the book. 'This is very funny. Sit down'. He took hold of her arm, drew her
down beside him. 'I want to read to you. Suppose they had won. What would it be like?
We don't have to worry; this man has done all the thinking for us'.
Philip K. Dick, *The Man in the High Castle*

**The first chapter of Rosalind Krauss's book *Passages in Modern Sculpture* begins with a
description of a scene from Eisenstein's film *October*. It is the opening scene and starts
with the camera exploring in detail a statue of Czar Nicholas II, ending with a crowd
bursting into the square that the statue occupies, fixing ropes around the statue and
dragging it to the ground. This act of iconoclasm through which Eisenstein celebrates
the coming of a new age and which Krauss uses as a way of arriving at a view of Rodin,
has become once again familiar this last year. But what would it be like if it were the
other way around, if we had witnessed the triumph of soviet communism? Crowds on
the streets of Hamburg, Cologne and Bonn. Queues of people desperate to enter East
Germany, Austrians flocking into Poland and Hungary. A wild night in Berlin when the
wall came down. Disintegration of the European Community and NATO. The United
States swiftly reduced to independent republics – Utah, Alaska, Texas, California,
Hawaii, The Confederacy, Navajo, Crow, Dakota. The Union itself a small group of
North Eastern states and Maryland (…)**

**The crowds have burst into the square, the symbols of an out-moded authority are
being thrown to the ground. What are they? Does the Washington monument totter? Is
the Lincoln memorial destroyed? The Statue of Liberty blown up? Perhaps it would only
be a matter of overturning a few police cars. Or maybe the works of Oldenburg, Serra,
Moore, Picasso, Miró?**

Lynne Cooke, 30 March, 1992
What would it mean for the works of Oldenburg, Serra, Moore, Picasso and Miró to survive
desecration and destruction unlike, say, the statues of Lenin, Stalin and others? Would it
indicate that their meanings are porous, that they are malleable and hence capable of a
rereading or manipulation, that, in short, they are politically correctable in the way that
the national flags flying in Bucharest in December 1990 were filleted, their central symbols
cut out leaving only the country's colours surrounding gaping holes? Would it mean that
they could remain present as monuments if they were, as signs, rendered (or considered)

mute? In a celebrated dictum now perhaps hackneyed but nonetheless pertinent, Robert Musil contended that a monument is immune to public attention and thus invisible. A monument in his definition is not, therefore, a sign (...)

During the Cold War the United States Government used Abstract Expressionist painting as a cultural weapon to further spread its political ideology. Today, multinational corporations do a far more effective job utilizing advertising signage. Perhaps it is inconceivable that when the crowds burst into the squares – Piccadilly Circus, or Times Square, say – that their first targets will prove to be the spectacolour boards devoted to Coke, Sony, and Marlboro ... But, almost certainly, Alfred Gilbert's *Eros*, like the statue of Father Francis P. Duffy on 42nd Street in New York City, will be bypassed in the excitement, ignored, unremarked ...

Richard Deacon, 2 April, 1992

'Now, Kitty, let's consider who it was that dreamed it all. This is a serious question, my dear, and you should not go on licking your paw like that – as if Dinah hadn't washed you this morning! You see, Kitty, it must have been either me or the Red King. He was part of my dream, of course – but then I was part of his dream, too!'
Lewis Carroll, *Through the Looking Glass*

It's interesting to suppose that the reasons for the United States government supporting Abstract Expressionist paintings are the very same reasons that our crowds might ignore the works of Picasso, Serra, Moore, Oldenburg, Miró etc. That is, the individuality, privacy, hermeticism, idiosyncrasy, even apparent meaninglessness of those works. It's contradictory isn't it? On the one hand a patronage, based in ideology, that understands freedom or liberty – high order values – as being expressed by the, if you like, extreme pursuit of individuality, of privacy. On the other hand something like ineffability, porosity in your word. Thus at the time of the bombing of Pan Am flight 103 over Lockerbie in 1988, one appalled commentator, desperately seeking ways of describing the scene of mindless destruction which confronted him, said of the twisted fragments of metal scattered across the ground that they were 'like modern sculpture' (...)
These are certainly questions about meaning, but they are also about 'public'. Thus we started by my description of the car, an interlocutor, in your phrase, in the corporate plaza, occupying a place that might be taken by an art work. The one precedes the other and, in general, it is publicness of space which is thought of as the container for works of art in public. But what if this were not the case, what if it were the other way round – that

left, Juan Muñoz
Untitled
1992
Jubilee Gardens, London

above, **Jochen Gerz and**
Esther Shalev-Gerz,
The Monument Against Fascism
1986-93

left, **Juan Muñoz**
Untitled
1992
Jubilee Gardens, London

it was 'publicness' in the art work which enabled a space to be public?

Lynne Cooke, 6 April, 1992

The question of whether the publicness is brought into being in and through the object, or whether it preexists it and pertains to the space itself brings up the issue of the relationship between the modernist sculpture, the monument and the memorial. It's my hunch that the monument and the memorial being recognizable and identifiable typologies in themselves are integrally public in address whereas the proper home of the autonomous modernist sculpture is the museum, for there self-referentiality is most securely in place. When it is placed outdoors the modernist sculpture seems to require that the site be read as an extension of the museum, as, in effect, a surrogate museum space of the kind exemplified in a sculpture park. In such venues the forms of address are implicitly in place before the work is encountered. By contrast when the character of the space is not sharply designated or where it has a hybrid identity, as in a corporate atrium, the work often runs the danger of being commandeered, and forced into embellishing the site and/or the patron (...)

Recently it has functioned in both active and passive ways, that is, firstly in ways that attempt to counter the loss of meaning, and secondly in ways that seek to profit from it. The gradually disappearing column, *Hamburg Monument Against Fascism*, which Jochen Gerz and Esther Shalev-Gerz constructed in Hamburg and that will ultimately become invisible is an instance of the former. The converse is found in a recent work by Juan Muñoz. This is a seemingly anonymous cenotaph, a memorial devoid of inscription, erected on the banks of the Thames in London. Modelled along the lines of the well known example of this monument found nearby, Muñoz's work was designed to meld directly into its milieu in such a way as to become virtually unnoticeable from the moment of its inception (...)

Richard Deacon, 17 April, 1992

Baudelaire's assumption, expressed negatively in his Salon criticism of 1846 ('tiresome') and positively in his Salon criticism of 1859 ('divine role') was that sculpture was necessarily primitive and close to nature: that is to say, incapable of becoming civilized, as painting is, without losing necessity and virtue. A central plank of Rilke's interest in and writing about Rodin was puzzlement bordering on awe that something made as art could dispense with its maker and exist in the world of things. Judd in his text _Specific Objects_ suggests the possibility of an art which borders on the ordinary and the matter of fact. This 'like 1, 2, 3' is a way of seeing the world. For all three of these writers, despite vast differences, the object is situated in the world where the subjectivity of the

spectator is engaged. This is a limit for Baudelaire, a source of existential questioning for Rilke and a means of demystification for Judd. It is without question for any of them that both the site of engagement is in the world and that what is engaged is the product of a human agent. There is no question of privacy. Whatever it is that all these three writers are considering, whether or not we want to call it sculpture, is in public, out there in the world. Like language it is neither yours nor mine and also like language, it is uncontained. What 'it' is and what constitutes 'the world' may not always be quite so clear.

I don't subscribe to Henry Moore's suggestions that the proper place for sculpture is outside. No more do I believe that the 'proper home of the autonomous modernist sculpture is the museum'. That seems to put the cart before the horse to me and carries with it a whiff of the prescriptive that I cannot let pass. This may be a matter of dogma to me, I don't know, since I recognize the truth, Lynne, in your comments about the sculpture park and the corporate atrium (…)

I've often begun discussions about my work by telling the following joke, it helps to break the ice.
Q. What do you get if you cross a centipede with a parrot?
A. A walkie-talkie.

I don't know how it is in French, but in English I find the compression wonderful. The question brings together two unlike organisms whose commonality is revealed by the answer. The two first organisms, one an insect (a creepy crawly) and the other a bird, are functionally anthropomorphized (anything with a 'hundred' feet can do nothing but walk, we repeat what we have learnt 'parrot fashion' as if talking could be divorced from understanding). The two single actions are very specific and the conjunction of walking and talking is somehow special. Their focus in the popular name of an artefact brings it, Pygmalion like, to life – 'she's a walking, talking, living doll' (Adam Faith – *Living Doll*). The combination of nature and culture thus achieved is very particularly human and language is the medium and the mechanism by which the conjunction is wrought. There is an external frame, a public net, provided by language yet it is within our own consciousnesses that understanding and appreciation takes place. We may laugh together but the cause of the laughter is deep within our own psyches. Thus it seems to me, the joke is an example of criss-crossing of not only categories of things but also of the barrier between the self and the world, where world is meant in the sense that it is a place occupied by human speakers (…)

Richard Deacon, Editions du Regard, Paris, 1992

Between Fiction and Fact
1992
Mild steel
480 × 1155 × 360 cm
Collection, Musée d'art moderne
Villeneuve d'Ascq

What You See Is What You Get 1992

... 'Oh Kitty! how nice it would be if we could only get through into Looking-glass House! I'm sure it's got, oh! such beautiful things in it! Let's pretend there's a way of getting through into it somehow, Kitty. Let's pretend the glass has got soft like gauze, so that we can get through. Why, it's turning into a sort of mist now, I declare! It'll be easy enough to get through —' She was up on the chimney piece while she said this, though she hardly knew how she had got there. And certainly the glass was beginning to melt away, just like a bright silvery mist.'
Lewis Carroll, *Through the Looking Glass*

One of the things that I really liked about the Vechte at Nordhorn, from the first time I visited, was that it reminded me of a stretch of the river Stour I had known well as a boy. The Stour, in some ways a much more rural river, ran through the water meadows. Weeds and lilies floated on its surface, pulled by the current. We children swam in the deep water just above the weir. It was only ever the sunlit surface that was warm, underneath the river ran on cold and dark, weeds occasionally wrapping your legs like a warning if you dived down deep beneath the surface. Below the weir, the river divided in two, one half slow and steady going on into the flour mill, where it drove the grinding wheels before falling turbulently into the mill pond and drifting out to join its other half which all the while had been rushing and bouncing along. I preferred this quicker half, the water was shallower, you could see more – especially from the cattlebridge. Leaning over the rails you could watch the swinging weeds and the darting life in the eddying river below. The mill reach was always dark, overshadowed by chestnut trees along the bank and which the surface reflected back, black against the sky. At the end of the reach the river plunged mysteriously through a grill into the noisy mill. This grill kept the largest floating debris from interfering with the machinery turning the grinding wheels as the water passed through the mill. The track from the village led over the water meadows, crossed the lower branch of the river and passed by the mill itself on a walkway over this grill. It was always interesting to look down and see what flotsam had been creamed off the water's surface, mostly twigs and branches but also bits of crates and boxes and, occasionally, dead fish. Once there was a dead cat. There were two other bridges in the water meadows, curiously abandoned, bridges over nothing, but whose purpose became clear when the winter floods made the river spread across the water meadows, reopening old pathways for itself. Then these bridges kept the track to the mill open.

     Summer mornings I could never sleep and would go out, leaving the sleeping

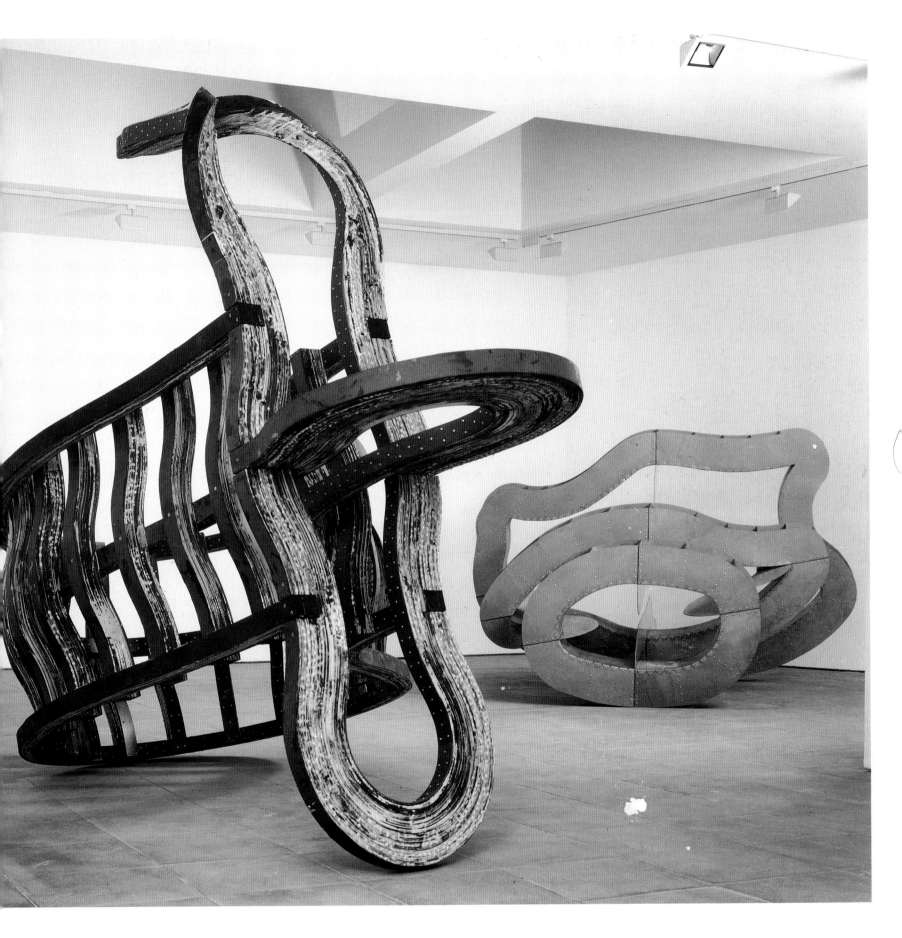

Installation, Lisson Gallery,
London
1987
l. to r., **Troubled Water**, 1987; **Fish
Out of Water**, 1986-87; **Feast for
the Eye**, 1986-87

house and walking across the wet fields to the river. Fish interested me. I was endlessly fascinated by the grey shapes I could see flitting from clump to clump of the weed beds or, on a hot afternoon, floating in the sunlit surface water. I'd begun to learn that different patches of water had different inhabitants; nervous dace darting where the water was shallow and ran rippling over the bed; roach in slightly deeper water, running in the channels between the weeds, the weeds themselves flicking lazily to and fro as the current swung and eddied; perch where the water was deeper still and the brown river began to hide the bottom; pike lurking in the deepest waters, prowling amongst the stems of the lily pads, an unseen, hunting presence advertised by the occasional panicky eruption of tiny fish from the surface.

I was often fishing. I wasn't much good at it and later gave it up because I no longer liked it, but at the time I was keen. One morning, in a favourite spot I began to notice a fish different from the rest just visible in the dark patch under some floating weeds, hanging back but occasionally snapping something floating past. Finally recognizing it as a brown trout – the roundels I could make out on its back were a giveaway – I began to fish for it. It was a discovery, the fish seemed to be a secret which I wanted to unlock. Every morning I would be up and out trying every bait I knew or had heard of, wet flies, worms, maggots, larvae, minnows, bread, cheese; a whole diet drifted past the fish's nose. Occasionally it would grab at something, only to spit the baited hook out almost instantly. My tackle got lighter and lighter until finally there was just a light line and a tiny hook with whatever bait I was trying floating down the river whilst I tried to keep contact without jerking the line. Finally catching the fish made me proud, but was also perhaps disappointing. The connection that I had made between out of the water and in the water had been electrifying, almost as if I'd been talking, but with the fish in my hand it was gone. I'd lost the guide that carried me into the river.

In the film, *The War of the Worlds*, at one point the optical extension of one of the Martian invaders is linked to a video monitor. 'Now let's see what a Martian sees!' says one of the actors, as if seeing and cognition were separated acts. One of my favourite school textbook diagrams used to be that which explained the fish eye view. The fish looking upwards, out of the water, is only able to see through the surface within a narrow circle. Beyond that circle light is internally reflected and an image of the river or sea bottom replaces that of the bank or shore. The fish has a window which moves around with it. The greater the depth the smaller the window. Similarly from the land, looking down from above the water can be seen through whereas at an acute angle the water reflects rather than refracts light and an image of sky, clouds, trees – the surroundings – appears in the surface. These of course are mechanical explanations, fish might as well be Martians. Nevertheless what's interesting about this textbook diagram is the notion that the surface is *occasionally* transparent, *occasionally* penetrable, depending on viewpoint. My hunting the trout seemed to involve opening that window through the surface.

Surface is both the extent of our looking and that which constitutes appearance. How do I look? is the question we ask others of ourselves. The body is at the same time behind the appearance, its substance. *The Man with the X-Ray Eyes* changed his receptivity to the electromagnetic spectrum by means of a chemical treatment, eye drops. In optical examination eye drops are often used to dilate the pupil and the feeling afterwards is often of too much light entering the eye, of somehow seeing too much, so

Feast for the Eye
1986-87
Galvanized steel
100 × 80 × 350 cm

One Step, Two Step
1992
Stainless steel
Commissioned by Stadt Nordhorn,
Germany
Landspitze

there is some logic to the use of eye drops as the means of expanding the range of perception. To begin with the treatment has salacious results – at a party it appears to him that no-one is wearing any clothes. Then this increased capacity becomes a diagnostic miracle as he is able to look through a girl's skin and detects the presence of a malignant but operable tumour. After an accident he is stripped of his research funding and outcast both from the hospital and from the scientific community. Isolated and alone he continues the dosage that transforms his vision, earning money in a circus performing tricks of mind reading, a mental freak. Finally and tragically he can no longer see anything except colour and pattern since there is no longer any barrier to his vision. He sees everything and nothing, receptivity destroys all objects, there are no longer any surfaces. There is no more world. The marvellous membrane which is the water surface seems to me to be on the edge of appearance, an outerlimit of objecthood. It's another world down there.

Installing **One Step, Two Step**
1992

> *I see a black bird up a tree,*
> *I see him and he sees me...*
> (Traditional song)

The second thing to try and write about at Nordhorn is why two? In some ways the proposal to have two parts to the work is a fairly natural development from being interested in the water. The original site, Landspitze, is the point where two streams of the same river meet. Since there is a point where they come together, there is also a place where they part. To me this was an immediate question – where does the stream split? A connection was always clear though the consequences of making the connection were not. In many ways the two places, Neumarkt where the stream splits and Landspitze where the two streams reconnect, allow a between, make a space, a before and after, a beginning and end. Nordhorn lies *between* the two points. I'm only a tourist so it's fair to say that this is a Nordhorn of mind, something that I have imagined. Nevertheless this Nordhorn is a single place, a node or fixed point in space. The river on the other hand is clearly in both places, Landspitze and Neumarkt, at the same time. It is not therefore fixed in space. A visitor is always only ever in one place at one time and a part of the experience of the work lies in going from one part to the other. In going from one to the other the work becomes confused with the visitor's experience, a combination of that which comes from the place and that which is brought to it.

'One Step ... Two Step' (cat.), Stadtgalerie Nordhorn, 1994

Replacing
1987
Set design for Rambert Dance Co.

Factory 1993

Factory
1993
Set design for Marietta Secret

Reading: A Propos de Toni Grand 1993

In Mircea Eliade's book Myth & Reality *one chapter is titled, 'Time Can be Overcome'. It is a basic purpose of mythic ritual and sacrament to overcome time. Horselover Fat found himself thinking in a language used two thousand years ago, the language in which St. Paul wrote. 'Here time turns into space' (Wagner, Parsifal). Fat told me another feature of his encounter with God: all of a sudden the landscape of California, USA, 1974 ebbed out and the landscape of Rome of the first century C.E. ebbed in. He experienced a superimposition of the two for a while, like techniques familiar in movies. In photography. Why? How? God explained many things to Fat but he never explained that, except for this cryptic statement: it is journal listing #3. 'He causes things to look different so it would appear time has passed'. Who is 'he'? Are we to infer that time has not in fact passed? And did it ever pass? Was there once a real time, and for that matter a real world, and now there is counterfeit time and a counterfeit world, like a sort of bubble growing and looking different but actually static?*

Horselover Fat saw fit to list this statement early in his journal or exegesis or whatever he calls it. Journal listing #4, the next entry goes:
'Matter is plastic in the face of the Mind'.
Phillip K. Dick, *Valis*

Fish is different from meat. Except for tuna. I've seen Japanese fishmongers, working in the big market in Tokyo changing the frozen carcasses of tuna into meat. The conversion is done by progressively slicing into smaller pieces. The frozen bodies are difficult to handle, heavy and awkwardly shaped, slipping a bit on the band saw bench. The first cut is longwise, into halves, the saw blade passing to one side of the back bone. After this it's easier, there's a flat surface to run on the saw table. The next cut is also longwise, quartering the body. Thereafter the cuts go across, producing blocks about as long as they are deep or a bit longer. These go into the fridges of other dealers and are sliced smaller and smaller as they thaw and as the fish is sold, red chunks, blocks and cubes; splinters of the whole body.

The second time I saw tunny, many years later, was in Spain on the Basque coast. This time it was a smaller species, Thunnus alalunga, which the French call germon *and the Americans* albacore, *the prized white tunny, the only one allowed to be sold as white meat tunny in the USA. Fat fisherwomen were pulling these tight skinned shapes over the quays of the small port of Llanes. Natural slime and blood greased the way so that they survived the brutal handling unblemished. We did not eat tunny for dinner that night.*

Next day we were glad to blot out that over-truthful image with a visit to the cave of Pindal where a palaeolithic tunny swims gracefully on the wall. One has to step up on to a stone to make out the engraved lines. And all the time the smell of sea and wild flowers hangs about the cave. I suppose that women have been lugging these meaty, full skinned fish over the ground hereabouts for 25,000 years and longer.
Jane Grigson, *Fish Cookery*, p. 201–202

At dusk in the autumn months starlings congregate in large numbers, chattering loudly and chaotically from their roost. All at once the whole flock will erupt skywards, joining other flocks forming a vast congregation swirling around the sky. The organization of these enormous numbers seems inexplicable. What keeps the flock together? Why don't they crash into one another? What is the significance of the elaborately changing patterns in the vibrant mass? As the light fades, the display stops as suddenly as it has begun and the birds return chirping and muttering to their perches for the night. Watching, there is a sense that these patterns can be read, as a sign of tomorrow's

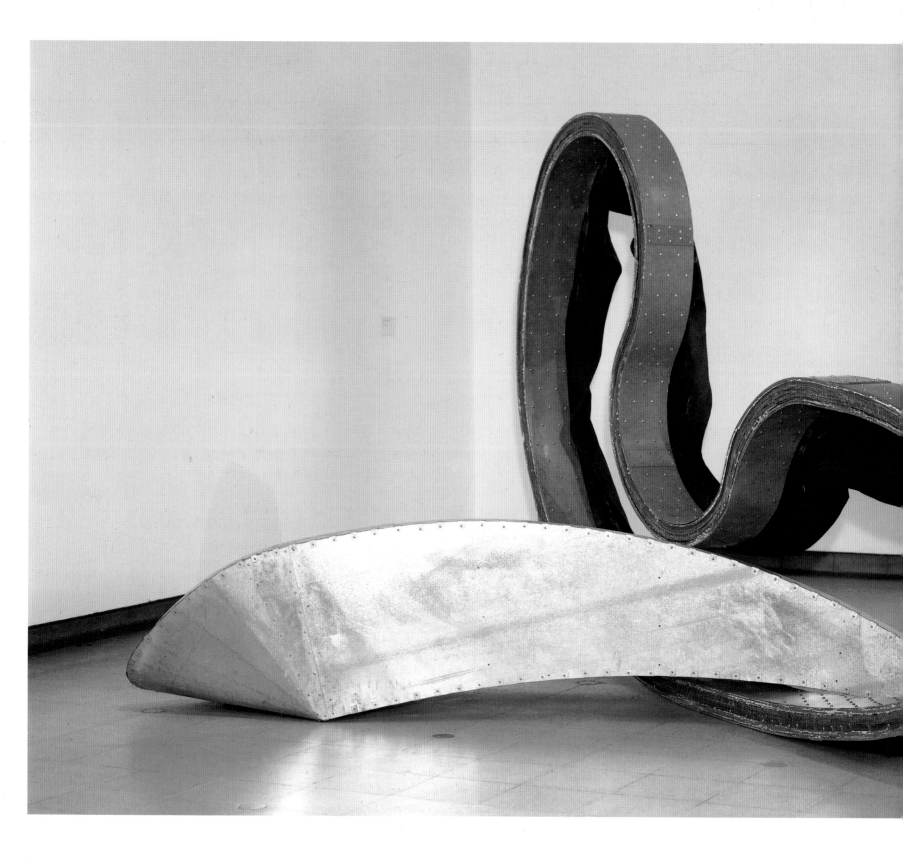

This, That and the Other
1985
Laminated hardboard, canvas,
galvanized steel
230 × 400 × 190 cm
Collection, Tate Gallery, London

weather perhaps or as a portent. They can be scanned, as we scan the clouds, for images to read, as are tea leaves in a cup, for clues to the future. The great silver shoals of herring that once occurred in the North Sea must have inspired similar musings. Where have they come from? Where are they going? What can they tell us? On land, the wildebeest wandering across the Serengeti plain form the last awesome herd that ebbs and flows with this same mysterious organization, the individual by virtue of number reduced to a particle in a fluctuating pattern.

Pattern is evidence of structure – at all levels from the twist of DNA to spiralling galaxies we read pattern as the evidence or consequence of structure; of forces, laws or interactions. Thus we infer that pattern in the flock, shoal or herd must in some way be consequent. This habit is very hard to break. A part of the difficulty is the specifics of the particles. Animals, fish or birds are volitional in ways that we don't believe stars or genetic material to be, so that in seeing pattern (and this is particularly so in collections of vast numbers) it is that much harder not to treat it as evidence of 'grand design'. Or as a sort of communication. The intensity of this difficulty, of the relationship between the part and the whole, is provocative in the work of Toni Grand, a provocation that is intensified by the absolute precision of titling adopted in the works of 1988-92 – *Sans titre* followed by a date, day, month, year. The relatively simple structures of these works are formed from units of great particularity – individual fish – units whose identity is almost erased by the encrusting resin. At Knaresborough, near Harrogate in West Yorkshire is the cave of Mother Shipton, a local hermit and prophet of some (eighteenth century) repute. In the cave various objects have been (and still are) put under the drips of water continually seeping through cracks in the limestone pavement above. The leached calcium comes out of solution and gradually encrusts the objects. The process is continuous, so that the oldest of them are by now little more than peculiarly shaped lumps, their identity effaced. In the more recent both the lump and its underlying object are visible, a kind of double, one becoming the other. The activity of the prophet pushes forward in time, reading into the future. The steady drip of the calcifying water marks the passage of the future into the past 'Here time turns into space' (or matter). Such doubles seem to be an essential component in the sculpture of Toni Grand, whether in the individual components; in the relation of part to whole; of structure to design; of object to matter; or of time to space.

'Toni Grand' (cat.), Musee Jeu de Paume, Paris; Camden Arts Centre, London, 1994

Art for Other People No 30
Rigid polythene
13 × 60 × 23 cm

Artist's Writings

Contents

Interview Pier Luigi Tazzi in conversation with **Richard Deacon**, page 6.   **Survey** Jon Thompson

Thinking Richard Deacon, Thinking Sculptor, Thinking Sculpture, **page 36.**   **Focus** Peter Schjeldahl Deacon's Faith,

page 88. **Artist's Choice** Mary Douglas Purity and Danger, 1966, **page 98.** **Artist's**

Writings Richard Deacon Selections from Stuff Box Object, 1971-72, **page 110.**   Artist's Statement, 1982, **page 114.**

Silence, Exile, Cunning, 1986-88, **page 116.**   What Car? Correspondence with Lynne Cooke, 1992 **page 120.**   What You See Is What

You Get, 1992, **page 132.**   Design for *Replacing*, 1987, **page 138.**   Design for *Factory*, 1993, **page 139.**   Reading: a propos de Toni

Grand, 1993, page 140.   **Chronology** **page 144** & Bibliography, **page 158.**

Chronology Richard Deacon Born 1949 in Bangor, Wales. Lives and works in London

Exhibitions and projects
1968-81

1968
Foundation Course, Somerset College of Art, Taunton
(Teachers incl. John Hilliard, Ian Breakwell, Rose Finn-
Kelcey)

1969-72
B.A. Sculpture, **St Martin's School of Art**, London
(Teachers incl. Peter Kardia, William Tucker, Garth
Evans, Gareth Jones)

1970
'New Arts Lab'
London, performance with C. Walters and I. Kirkwood
(group)

'Stuff Box Object', **St Martin's School of Art**, London
Re-edited and published as catalogue by the Chapter
Arts Centre, Cardiff, 1984

1972 - 73
Students and staff of St Martin's, form 'Manydeed'
group to provide forum for collective activities and
meetings

1972
Essex University (performance) (group)

1973
Travels through USA, attends Grotowski's acting
classes, Art Institute of Chicago

1974
'Artists' Meeting Place',
London (performance with Manydeed group) (group)

1974-77
M.A. Environmental Media, Royal College of Art (under
Peter Kardia), London

1975/76
Royal College of Art Galleries, London (solo)

1977
Text, 'Notes on a piece of Sculpture', *Royal College of
Art Journal*, No 1

Studies History of Art, **Chelsea School of Art**, London

Teaching, **Central School of Art**, London (-1983)

1978
'Studio Exhibition',
The Gallery, Brixton, London (solo)

1978-79
Lives and works in New York

1980
'Spring Programme',
The Gallery, Brixton, London (solo)

Teaching, **Sheffield Polytechnic** (-1984)

1981
Sheffield City Polytechnic Gallery, Sheffield (solo)
Text, exhibition catalogue,*Jacqui Poncelet, New
Ceramics*, Craft Council

Selected articles and interviews
1968-81

Sack Event, Somerset College of Art, March 1969

Project with Andrew Rice, St Martin's School of Art, 1971

'A Course', St Martin's School of Art, 1972

Performance, Richard Deacon and Clive Walters,
May 1972

1980
Cooke, Lynne, 'Carolyne Kardia at Felicity Samuel,
Richard Deacon at The Gallery, Brixton', *Artscribe*,
London, No 24

1981

Exhibitions and projects
1981-83

'Objects and Sculpture',
(Allington, Deacon, Gormley, Kapoor, Organ, Randall-Page, Vilmouth, Woodrow)
Institute of Contemporary Art, London, **Arnolfini Gallery**, Bristol (group)
Cat. *Objects and Sculpture*, ICA, London and Arnolfini Gallery, Bristol, text Lewis Biggs, Sandy Nairne, Iwona Blazwick, interviews with the artists

1982
Teaching, **Bath Academy of Arts** (-1985), **Chelsea School of Art**, London (continues)

'Englische Plastik Heute/British Sculpture Now',
Kunstmuseum, Luzern, Switzerland (group)
Cat. *Englische Plastik Heute/British Sculpture Now*, Kunstmuseum, Luzern, Switzerland, texts Martin Kunz and Michael Newman

'Objects and Figures: New Sculpture in Britain',
Fruitmarket Gallery, Edinburgh, organized by the Scottish Arts Council touring to **John Hansard Gallery**, Southampton (group)
Cat. *Objects and Figures: New Sculpture in Britain*, The Scottish Arts Council, Edinburgh, text Michael Newman

1983
Lisson Gallery,
London (solo)

The Orchard Gallery, Derry, Northern Ireland (solo)
Cat. *Richard Deacon: Sculpture*, The Orchard Gallery, Derry, text Lynne Cooke

'New Art',
Tate Gallery, London (group)
Cat. *New Art*, Tate Gallery, London, text Michael Compton

'The Sculpture Show',
Hayward and Serpentine Galleries, London (group)
Cat. *The Sculpture Show*, Hayward and Serpentine Galleries, London, texts Kate Blacker, Fenella Crichton, Paul De Monchaux, Nena Dimitrijevic, Stuart Morgan, Deanna Petherbridge, Bryan Robertson and Nicholas Wadley

'Transformations: New Sculpture from Britain,'
XVII Bienal de Sao Paulo, Brazil, organized by the British Council toured to **Museo de Arte Moderna**, Rio de Janeiro; **Museo de Arte Moderna**, Mexico, **Fundacao Calouste Gulbenkien**, Lisbon (group)
Cat. *Transformations: New Sculpture from Britain*, The British Council, London, texts Lynne Cooke, John Roberts, Nicholas Serota, Lewis Biggs, Stuart Morgan, Mark Francis and John McEwan

Installation, Objects and Sculptures, Institute of Contemporary Arts, London, 1981

Selected articles and interviews
1981-83

Francis, Mark, 'Objects & Sculpture', *Art Monthly*, London, No 48
Roberts, John, 'Objects & Sculpture', *Artscribe*, London, No 30
Biggs, Lewis, 'Objects & Sculpture', *Arnolfini Review*, Bristol, June/July

1982

Fisher, Peter, 'Moore und die Erben - Die Neue Englische Plastik', *Nurnberger Zeitung*, Nurnberg, 12 June
Faure-Walker, Caryn, 'Interview with Richard Deacon', *Aspects*, London, No 17
Newman, Michael, 'New Sculpture in Britain', *Art in America*, New York, September

1983
Cooke, Lynne, 'Richard Deacon: Lisson Gallery', *Art Monthly*, London, No 64
Miller, Sanda, 'Richard Deacon, Galerie Lisson', *Art Press*, Paris, No 70

Donnely, Micky, 'Richard Deacon Sculpture', Orchard Gallery, *Circa*, Dublin, No 11

Newman, Michael, 'Figuren en Objecten', *Museum Journaal*, Amsterdam, No 2
Cooke, Lynne, 'Reconsidering the New Sculpture', *Artscribe*, London, No 42

Exhibitions and projects
1984-85

1984
Riverside Studios, London (solo)

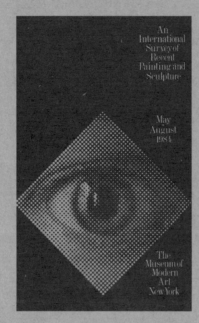

Chapter Arts Centre, Cardiff (solo)
Cat. *Stuff Box Object, Richard Deacon 1972/73*, Chapter
Arts Centre, Cardiff, text Richard Deacon

'Richard Deacon: Sculpture 1980-1984',
Fruitmarket Gallery, Edinburgh
toured to **Le Nouveau Musée**, Lyon/Villeurbanne (solo)
Cat. *Richard Deacon. Sculpture 1980-84*, Fruitmarket
Gallery, text Michael Newman

'Turner Prize Exhibition',
Tate Gallery, London (group)

'An International Survey of Recent Painting and
Sculpture', **Museum of Modern Art**, New York (group)
Cat. *An International Survey of Recent Painting and
Sculpture*, Museum of Modern Art, New York, text
Kynaston McShine

1985
'Contemporary Sculpture',
Donald Young Gallery, Chicago (solo)

'Nouvelle Biennale de Paris',
Paris (group)

'Five Recent Sculptures',
Tate Gallery, London (solo)
Cat. *Richard Deacon, Talking About Those Who Have Ears
No 2 and Other Works*, Patrons of New Art, Tate Gallery,
London, interview Richard Francis

'Beyond Appearances. Sculpture for the visually
handicapped and sighted to share',
Castle Museum, Nottingham (group)

'Three British Sculptors: Richard Deacon, Julian Opie,
Richard Wentworth',
The Israel Museum, Jerusalem (group)

'Place Saint Lambert Investigations',
Espace Nord, Liège, Belgium (group)

'Blind, Deaf and Dumb',
An installation in collaboration with Richard Rogers

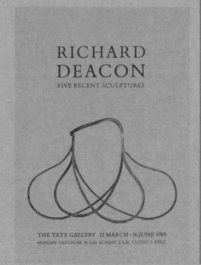

Selected articles and interviews
1984-85

1984
Januszczak, Waldemar, 'Richard Deacon', *The
Guardian*, London, 7 February
Miller, Sanda, 'Richard Deacon', *Art Press*, Paris, No 80
Collier, Caroline, 'Richard Deacon at the Riverside
Studios', *Studio International*, London, vol 196, No
1004
Cooke, Lynne, 'Richard Deacon at the Riverside
Studios', *Art in America*, New York, September
McEwan, John, 'London Round up, Richard Deacon',
Art in America, New York, November

Newman, Michael, 'Discourse and Desire, Recent
British Sculpture', *Flash Art*, Milan, January
Newman, Michael, 'Le Spectacle de la Melancolie dans
la Consommation de Masse: Signification et Objectifs
dans la Sculpture Britannique Actuelle', *Artistes*,
France, No 18
Dimitrijevic, Nena, 'Sculpture after Evolution', *Flash
Art*, Milan, April/May

1985
Kirshner, Judith Russi, 'Tony Cragg, Richard Deacon at
Donald Young Gallery, Chicago', *Artforum*, New York,
Summer

'Maison de Verre. Blind, Deaf and Dumb', *Building
Design*, London, 4 October

Exhibitions and projects
1985-86

and John Tchalenko, **Serpentine Gallery**, London
(solo)
'Wall of Light', film made in collaboration with Richard
Rogers and John Tchalenko

'1985 Carnegie International',
Carnegie Museum of Art, Carnegie Institute,
Pittsburgh (group)
Cat. *1985 Carnegie International*, Carnegie Museum of
Art, anthology, introduction Jack Lane and John
Caldwell

'Transformations in Sculpture: Four Decades of
American and European Art',
Solomon R Guggenheim Museum, New York (group)
Cat. *Transformations in Sculpture: Four Decades of
American and European Art*, Solomon R. Guggenheim
Museum, text Diane Waldman

'The Poetic Object: Richard Deacon, Shirazeh
Houshiary and Anish Kapoor',
Douglas Hyde Gallery, Dublin, toured to **Arts Council
Gallery**, Belfast (group)
Cat. *The Poetic Object: Richard Deacon, Shirazeh
Houshiary and Anish Kapoor*, The Douglas Hyde Gallery,
Dublin, text Richard Francis

'The British Show',
toured to **Art Gallery of Western Australia**, Perth;
Gallery of New South Wales, Sydney; **Queensland Art
Gallery**, Brisbane; **The Exhibition Hall**, Melbourne;
National Art Gallery, Wellington, New Zealand)
(group)
Cat. *The British Show*, Art Gallery of New South Wales,
Sydney, text Waldemar Januszczak

1986
'Out of Line. Peter Moores Liverpool Project',
Walker Art Gallery, Liverpool (group)

'Skulptur-9 Kunstnere Fra Storbrittanien',
Louisiana Museum of Modern Art, Humlebaek,
Denmark (group)
Magazine, *Louisiana Revy*, various authors

'Falls the Shadow: Recent British and European Art',
Hayward Gallery, London (group)
Cat. *Falls the Shadow*, The Arts Council of Great Britain,
London, texts Barry Barker and Jon Thompson

'Entre el Objeto y la Imagen. Escultura Britanica
Contemporanea',
Palacio Velasquez, Madrid and **Fundacion Caja de
Pensiones**, Barcelona (group)
Cat. *Entre el Objeto y la Imagen. Escultura Britanica*

Selected articles and interviews
1985-86

Allthorpe-Guyton, Marjorie, 'Richard Deacon,
Serpentine Gallery', *Arts Review*, London, 25 October
Garlake, Margaret, 'Ruszkowski, Deacon, Jones',
Art Monthly, London, No 101

Richard Deacon and Tony Cragg, Chicago, Spring 1985

Lyn, Victoria, 'Six British Sculptors', *Art and Australia*,
Australia, December

Bickers, Patricia, 'A Conversation with Richard
Deacon', *Art Monthly*, London, No 83
Newman, Michael, 'Richard Deacon, La Face des
Choses', *Art Press*, Paris, March
Thompson, Jon, 'Richard Deacon in conversation with
Jon Thompson', *Lo Spazio Umano*, Milan, No 3,
August/September

1986
Hilton, Tim, 'Mixed Offering', *The Observer*, London, 2
February
Murdoch, Lothian, 'Peter Moores', *The Guardian*,
London, 12 February
Henri, Adrian, 'Figuring Out the Common
Denominator', *Daily Post*, London

Newman, Michael, 'Tigenes Ansigt. Tilgenet mindet om
min faber', *Louisiana Revy*, Denmark, 26/2, March

FALLS
THE
SHADOW
RECENT BRITISH
AND
EUROPEAN ART

THE HAYWARD ANNUAL
1986

Exhibitions and projects
1986-87

Contemporanea, The British Council and Ministerio de Cultura, Spain, texts Jon Thompson, Lewis Biggs and Juan Muñoz

'Sonsbeek 1986. International Sculpture Exhibition', Arnhem, The Netherlands (group)
Cat. *Sonsbeek 1986. International Sculpture Exhibition*, Arnhem, texts, Saskia Bos, Antje von Graevenitz, Mariannne Brouwer and contributing artists

'Prospect 86. Eine Internationale Austellung Aktueller Kunst', **Frankfurter Kunstverein**, Frankfurt (group)
Cat. *Prospect 86. Eine Internationale Austellung Aktueller Kunst*, Frankfurter Kunstverein, Frankfurt, text Peter Weiermair

'Correspondentie Europa',
Stedelijk Museum, Amsterdam (group)
Cat. *Correspondentie Europa*, Stedelijk Museum, Amsterdam, text Alexander Van Grevenstein

Marian Goodman Gallery, New York (solo)

'Sculpture for Exterior and Interior',
Interim Art, London (solo)

'For Those Who Have Eyes. Richard Deacon Sculptures 1980-86',
Aberystwyth Arts Centre, Wales, toured to **Glynn Vivian Gallery**, Swansea; **Turner House**, **National Museum of Wales**; **Mostyn Art Gallery**, Llandudno; **Warwick Art Centre**; **City Museum and Art Gallery**, Stoke on Trent (solo)
Cat. *For Those Who Have Eyes. Richard Deacon Sculptures 1980-86*, Aberystwyth Arts Centre, Wales, text Richard Deacon

Galerie Arlogos, Nantes, France (solo)
Cat. *Richard Deacon*, Galerie Arlogos, text Michel Enrici

1987
'A Quiet Revolution: British Sculpture Since 1965',
Museum of Contemporary Art, Chicago and **San Francisco Museum of Modern Art**, toured to **Newport Harbour Art Museum**, Newport Beach, California; **Hirshhorn Museum**, Washington; **Albright-Knox Art Gallery**, Buffalo (group)
Cat. *A Quiet Revolution: British Sculpture Since 1965*, Museum of Contemporary Art, Chicago and San Francisco Museum of Modern Art, text Mary Jane Jacob

'Current Affairs: British Painting and Sculpture in the 1980s',
Museum of Modern Art, Oxford, toured to

Selected articles and interviews
1986-87

Brenson, Michael, 'Richard Deacon at Marian Goodman', *New York Times*, 16 May
Cameron, Dan, 'Armleder, Martin, Deacon', *Flash Art*, Milan, No 130
Adams, Brook, 'Richard Deacon at Marian Goodman', *Art in America*, New York, January

Phillipson, Michael, 'Richard Deacon at Interim Art', *Artscribe*, London, January/February, 1987

Giquel, Pierre, 'Exposition Richard Deacon, Galerie Arlogos, Nantes', *Art Press*, Paris, February

Harrison, Charles, 'Sculpture, Design and Three-Dimensional Work', *Artscribe*, London, No 58
Newman, Michael, 'Fallen Haloes', *Artscribe*, London, No 58
Cooke, Lynne, 'Impresa', *Flash Art*, Milan, No 130
Cooke, Lynne, 'What is Modern Sculpture?', *Artscribe International*, London, No 60

1987

Exhibitions and projects
1987-88

Mucsarnok, Budapest; **National Gallery**, Prague; **Zachenta**, Warsaw (group)
Cat. *Current Affairs: British Painting and Sculpture in the 1980s*, Museum of Modern Art, Oxford, text Andrew Brighton

Lisson Gallery, London (solo)

'Britannia. Paintings and Sculptures from the 1980s', **Liljevalchs Konsthall**, Stockholm, organized by the British Council, toured to **Sara Hilden Art Museum**, Tampere, Finland (group)
Cat. *Britannia. Paintings and Sculptures from the 1980s*, The British Council, text Richard Francis, contributing artists

'Juxtapositions: Recent Sculpture from England and Germany',
PSI, The Institute for Art and Urban Resources Inc, New York (group)
Cat. *Juxtapositions: Recent Sculpture from England and Germany*, PSI, The Institute for Art and Urban Resources Inc, New York, texts Alanna Heiss and Joshua Decter

'Skulptur Projekte in Münster',
Münster (group)
Cat. *Skulptur Projekte in Münster*, text contrib. artists

Collaboration with Rambert Dance company, 'Replacing', choreographed by Lucy Bethune, performed at the **Riverside Studios**, London

'Turner Prize Exhibition',
Tate Gallery, London (group)

Awarded Turner Prize, London

'Richard Deacon. Recent Sculpture 1985-1988',
Bonnefanten Museum, Maastricht, toured to Kunstmuseum, Luzern; **Fundacion Caja de Pensiones**, Madrid; **Museum van Hedendaagse Kunst**, Antwerp (solo)
Cat. *Richard Deacon. Recent Sculpture 1985-1988*, Bonnefanten Museum, Maastricht, texts Charles Harrison, Alexander van Grevenstein and Martin Kunz

Installation, Bonnefanten Museum, Maastricht, 1987

1988
'The Analytical Theatre: New Art from Britain', organized by Independent Curators Inc., New York, toured to **The Akron Art Museum**, Ohio; **Alberta College Art Gallery**, Alberta; **University Art Museum**, California; **ICA**, Philadelphia (group)
Cat. *The Analytical Theatre: New Art from Britain*,

Selected articles and interviews
1987-88

Like a Snail, in progress, 1987

'The Critic's Way - Munster', *Artforum*, New York, September
Auty, Giles, 'The Stamp of Official Approval', *The Spectator*, London, 5 December

Tilroe, Anna, 'Deacon, Gijsbers en Schouten', *de Volkskrant*, Amsterdam, 27 November
Jarque, Fietta, 'Richard Deacon establece un dialogo continuo entre las esculturas y sus titulos', *El Pais*, Madrid, 11 April
Trenas, Miguel Ángel, 'Richard Deacon: Mis esculturas no esconden, permiten conocer su piel', *La Vanguardia*, Spain, 12 April
Dobbels, Daniel, 'Deacon, après le déluge', *Libération*, Paris, 18 April
'Richard Deacon: Disciplina Inglesa', *Epoca*, Madrid, 2 May

Baker, Kenneth, 'A Revolution in British Sculpture', *San Francisco Examiner*
Cornall, John, 'Very Like a Whale: Meaning in the Sculpture of Richard Deacon', *Alba*, No 6, Winter
Van Dorgu, Edna, 'Lectures on Sculpture', *De Appel*, Amsterdam, No 2
Cork, Richard, 'Cragg, Woodrow and Deacon: Three Individuals', *Arts and Design*, London, No 11/12

1988

Richard Deacon and George Melly at the Turner Prize presentation, 1987

Exhibitions and projects
1988

Independent Curators Incorporated, New York, text Michael Newman

Marian Goodman Gallery, New York (solo)
Cat. *Richard Deacon*, Marian Goodman Gallery, New York, text Peter Schjeldahl

'Schlaf Der Vernunft',
Museum Fridericianum, Kassel (group)
Cat. *Schlaf Der Vernunft*, Museum Fridericianum, Kassel, text Hubertus Gassner

The Carnegie Museum of Art, Pittsburgh, Pennsylvania toured to **The Museum of Contemporary Art**, Los Angeles and **Art Gallery of Ontario**, Toronto (solo)
Cat. *Richard Deacon*, The Carnegie Museum of Art, Pittsburgh, Pennsylvania, texts Richard Deacon, Lynne Cooke, Michael Newman, Peter Schjeldahl and John Caldwell

'Starlit Waters: British Sculpture, An International Art 1968-1988', **Tate Gallery**, Liverpool (group)
Cat. *Starlit Waters*, Tate Gallery, Liverpool, texts Lewis Biggs, Ian Chambers, Lynne Cooke, Richard Francis, Charles Harrison, Martin Kunz

'Art in the Garden: The Glasgow Garden Festival 1988', Glasgow (group)
Cat. *Art in the Garden Installations*, The Glasgow Garden Festival 1988, Edinburgh, text Graham Murray

'Rosc '88',
Guinness Hop Store, Dublin (group)
Cat. *Rosc '88*, Guinness Hop Store, Dublin, texts Patrick Murphy, Olle Granath and Aidan Dunne

'Brittanica: 30 ans de Sculpture',
Musée des Beaux Arts André Malraux, Le Havre; **Ecole d'Architecture de Normandie**, Rouen; **Musée de l'Evreux**; **Musee van Hedendaagse Kunst**, Antwerp (group)
Cat. *Brittanica: 30 ans de Sculpture*, Musée des Beaux Arts André Malraux, Le Havre; Ecole d'Architecture de Normandie, Rouen; Musée de l'Evreux, Evreux, texts Catherine Grenier, Françoise Cohen and Lynne Cooke

Whitechapel Art Gallery, London (solo)
Cat. *Richard Deacon*, Whitechapel Art Gallery, London, texts Lynne Cooke, Marjorie Allthorpe-Guyton and Catherine Lampert

Selected articles and interviews
1988

Brenson, Michael, 'Richard Deacon's Sculptures at the Marian Goodman Gallery', *The New York Times*, New York, 14 March

Studio, work in progress, 1988

Fonce, Jan, 'For Those Who Have Eyes', *Artefactum*, Belgium, September/October

Shone, Richard, London, 'Whitechapel. Sculpture by Richard Deacon', *Burlington Magazine*, London, February
Archer, Michael, 'Review, Whitechapel', *Art Monthly*, London, March
Feaver, William, 'Richard Deacon, Whitechapel Art Gallery', *ARTnews*, New York, April
Hatton, Brian, 'Richard Deacon, Whitechapel', London, *Flash Art*, Milan, May/June
Harrison, Charles, *Arts Magazine*, New York, No 109, March
Durand, Regis, 'Richard Deacon: le grand "fabricateur"', *Art Press*, Paris, 134
Hilton, Tim, 'A Visiting Aggression', *The Guardian*, London, 23 November
Graham-Dixon, Andrew, 'Riveting Stuff', *The Independent*, London, 3 December

Installation, Whitechapel Art Gallery, London, 1988

Exhibitions and projects
1988-90

'Richard Deacon. Distance No Object',
The Museum of Contemporary Art, Los Angeles (solo)

1989
'Richard III',
Galerie Arlogos, Nantes (group)

'Richard Deacon: 10 Sculptures 1987/89',
Musée d'art moderne de la Ville de Paris, Paris (solo)
Cat. *Richard Deacon: 10 Sculptures 1987/89*, Musée
d'art moderne de la Ville de Paris, Paris, texts Suzanne
Pagé and Jérôme Sans

'Sculpture Chicago '89',
Cityfront Center, Chicago (group)
Cat. *Sculpture Chicago '89*, Cityfront Center, text
John Neff

'Skulpturen fur Krefeld I',
Museum Haus Esters, Krefeld, Germany (group)
Cat. *Skulpturen fur Krefeld I*, Museum Haus Esters, text
Julian Heynen

1990
'Richard Deacon: Nye Arbeiter/New Works',
Kunstnernes Hus, Oslo (solo)
Artist's Book: *Atlas: Gondwanaland and Eurasia*,
Kunstnernes Hus, Oslo

Lecture, 'Contemporary Art Practice', Laing Art
Gallery, Newcastle upon Tyne

'Frank Auerbach, Lucian Freud, Richard Deacon',
The Saatchi Collection, London (group)
Cat. *Frank Auerbach, Lucian Freud, Richard Deacon*,
The Saatchi Collection, London, text Joanna Skipwith

'Sculpture',
Marian Goodman Gallery, New York (solo)
Galleria Locus Solus, Genoa (solo)

Lecture *M'ARS*, Ljubljana, Slovenia, Vol II, No. 4 ,
Summer

'British Art Now: A Subjective View',
organized by the British Council, toured to **Setagaya
Museum**, Tokyo; **Fukuoka Art Museum; Nagoya City
Museum; Tochigi Prefectural Museum of Fine Arts;
Hyogo Prefectural Museum; Hiroshima City Museum**
(group)
Cat. *British Art Now: A Subjective View*, The British
Council, texts Junichi Shioda, Andrew Graham-Dixon,
Akio Obigone

'New Works for Different Places: Four Cities Project',
Victoria Park, Plymouth (group)
Cat. *New Works for Different Places: Four Cities Project*,
TSWA - Four Cities Project, London/Plymouth, texts

SKULPTUREN FÜR KREFELD I

MUSEUM HAUS ESTERS KREFELD
3. SEPTEMBER - 22. OKTOBER 89

FRANK AUERBACH   LUCIAN FREUD
RICHARD DEACON

PREVIEW THURSDAY 22 MARCH 1990
6 to 9pm

SAATCHI COLLECTION
RSVP 98A BOUNDARY ROAD LONDON NW8 0RH TELEPHONE 01-624 8299

Selected articles and interviews
1988-90

Puvogel, Renate, 'Richard Deacon', *Kunstforum*,
Cologne, April/May, p.274
Anderson, Michael, 'Richard Deacon at the Museum of
Contemporary Art', *Art Issues*, Los Angeles, April 1989

Ferbos, Catherine, 'Sculptures in Between -
le paysage', *Artstudio*, Paris, Autumn
Paul, Frédéric, 'Richard Deacon, un exercise d'auto-
critique d'art', *Artstudio*, Paris, No 10

1989

Thomas, Mona, 'Richard Deacon: Portrait', *Beaux-Arts*
Paris, No 66
'L'interview Richard Deacon', *Art Press*, Paris, 134
Enrici, Michel, 'Richard Deacon: Un Pan de Labeur,
Inestimable', *Galeries Magazine*, Paris, No 30

'Richard Deacon', *Atelier*, Japan, October

1990

art press 134

Du situationnisme
au simulationnisme
Histoire d'une exposition :
finir en beauté
Les nouveaux horizons
de la Tate Gallery

L'art, l'homosexualité

Richard Deacon

Pack, in progress, 1990

Furse, John, 'Richard Deacon', *Art Monthly*, London,
No 132
Furse, John, 'TSWA: Plymouth Update', *Art Monthly*,
London, No 141
Usherwood, Paul, 'Deacon and Wodiczko on Tyneside',

Exhibitions and projects
1990-91

Tony Foster, Jonathan Harvey, James Lingwood

'Once upon a time...',
Former Redheugh Bridge Abutment, Gateshead,
England, commissioned by Gateshead Metropolitan
Borough Council

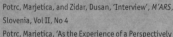

'Between the Eyes',
Yonge Square International Plaza, No 1 Yonge Street,
Toronto, commissioned by Camrost Developments
Corporation.

Moderna Galerija, Mala Galerija, Ljubljana, Slovenia
(solo)
Cat. *Richard Deacon*, Mala Galerija and Moderna
Galerija, Ljubljana, Slovenia, text Michael Newman

'Ambiguous Gestures',
lecture at University College London

'Weitersehen',
Museum Haus Esters and **Museum Haus Lange**,
Krefeld (group)
Cat. *Weitersehen*, Museum Haus Esters and Museum
Haus Lange, Krefeld, text Julian Heynen

1991
'Devil on the Stairs: Art from the 80s',
Institute of Contemporary Art, Philadelphia, toured
to **Newport Harbor Museum**, Newport Harbor (group)
Cat. *Devil on the Stairs: Looking Back on the Eighties*,
ICA Philadelphia, text Robert Storr in collaboration
with Judith Tannenbaum

'Skulpturen und Zeichnungen',
Museum Haus Lange and **Museum Haus Esters**,
Krefeld (solo)
Cat. *Richard Deacon*, Museum Haus Lange und Haus
Esters, Krefeld, interview Julian Heynen
'The Interior is Always More Difficult', 30 minutes,
VHS. Directed by Martin Kreyssig, produced by Richard
Deacon. Made for exhibition at Museum Haus Lange
and Haus Esters, Krefeld, Germany

'Inheritance and Transformation',
The Irish Museum of Modern Art, Dublin (group)
Cat. *Inheritance and Transformation*, The Irish Museum
of Modern Art, text Declan McGonagle and John
Hutchinson

'Nobody Here But Us',
Office Tower Plaza, 135 Albert Street, Auckland, New
Zealand, commissioned by ASB Properties Limited and
Albert Street Developments Limited

'Carnegie International 1991',
The Carnegie Museum of Art, Pittsburgh (group)
Cat. *Carnegie International 1991*, The Carnegie Museum
of Art, Pittsburgh, texts Philip Johnston, Lynne Cooke,
Mark Francis, Fumio Nanjo, Zinovy Zinik

Galerie Konrad Fischer, Düsseldorf (solo)

Installation, Carnegie International, 1991

Selected articles and interviews
1990-91

Usherwood, Paul, 'Deacon and Wodiczko on Tyneside',
Art Monthly, London, No 144, 1991

Potrc, Marjetica, and Zidar, Dusan, 'Interview', *M'ARS*,
Slovenia, Vol II, No 4
Potrc, Marjetica, 'As the Experience of a Perspectively
Arranged World Comes to an End', *M'ARS*, Slovenia, Vol
II, No 4

Jocks, Heinz-Norbert, 'Weitersehen', *Kunstforum*,
Germany, Bd.111, January/February

Private view at Mala Galerija, Ljubljana, 1990

Baker, Kenneth, 'Physical Precision, notes on some
recent sculpture', *Artspace*, September/October

1991

Frese, Hans Martin, 'Deacon in Krefeld', Von Laokoon
zu Theseus, *Rheinische Post*, Germany, 16 May
Meschede, Friedrich, 'Richard Deacon im Museum Haus
Lange/Haus Esters, Krefeld', *Kunst-Bulletin*, Germany,
July/August
Restorff, Jörg, 'Richard Deacon, Museen Haus Lange
und Esters, Krefeld', *Kunstforum*, Germany,
July/August

'Sculpture takes up its space', *New Zealand Herald*, 22
June

Kuoni, Carin, 'Pittsburgh: Carnegie International',
Kunstbulletin, Germany, December
Archer, Michael, 'Harmony and Dislocation', *Art
Monthly*, London, February, 1992

Exhibitions and projects
1991-92

'Drawings 1974-91'
Mead Gallery, University of Warwick, Coventry (solo)
Cat. *Let's Not Be Stupid*, texts Katherine Eustace and
Michael Newman

'Let's Not Be Stupid', Former Air Hall Site, University of
Warwick, Coventry, England
Commissioned by the University of Warwick

Text, 'A Sculptor's View, Living in a Material World',
essay in exhibition catalogue, *The Non-Objective World*,
South Bank Centre, London

1992
'Foursome',
Lisson Gallery, London (solo)

Let's Not Be Stupid, in progress, 1991

'Allegories of Modernism, Contemporary Drawing',
Museum of Modern Art, New York (group)
Cat. *Allegories of Modernism, Contemporary Drawing*,
Museum of Modern Art, New York, text Bernice Rose

'Three Recent Works',
The Economist Building Plaza, London (solo)

'Art for Other People',
Musée d'art moderne, Villeneuve d'Ascq, France (solo)
Cat. *Art for Other People*, Musée d'art moderne de la
Communité Urbaine de Lille, Villeneuve d'Ascq, texts
Joëlle Pijaudier and Jean De Loisy

'Between Fiction and Fact',
Musée d'art Moderne, Villeneuve d'Ascq
Commissioned by the Ministry of Culture and the Urban
Community of Lille, Villeneuve d'Ascq

'The Interior Is Always More Difficult',
Ecole Regionale d'Art de Dunkerque, Dunkerque (solo)

'Building from the Inside',
Voltaplatz, Krefeld, Germany
Commissioned by the Krefelder Kulturstiftung

'Platzverführung',
Kultur Region, Stuttgart (group)
Cat, *Platzeverführung*, Kultur Region, texts Rudi Fuchs,
Veit Gorner
Cat. *This Is Not a Story*, Stadt Waiblingen, Hugo
Mathaes, Verlag, Stuttgart

'Documenta IX',
Kassel

Selected articles and interviews
1991-92

Cork, Richard, 'Grand Motto for Life', *The Times*,
London, 4 February
Bickers, Patricia, 'Interview with Richard Deacon about
his Recent Pub.ic Sculpture', *Art Monthly*, London,
October

Cassim, Julia, 'Deacon's Tear Resonates', *The Japan
Times*, 16 June

1992
Cork, Richard, 'Guessing Games and Cheeky Jokes', *The
Times*, London, 14 February
Hall, James, 'Organs of Desire', *The Independent*,
London, 18 February
Bevan, Roger, 'Richard Deacon in London, Krefeld and
Pittsburgh', *Modern Painters*, London, Spring
'Richard Deacon', *Nikkei Art*, Japan, No 4
Dexter, Emma, 'United Kingdom, Richard Deacon,
Lisson Gallery', *Sculpture*, London, May/June

Schjeldahl, Peter, 'Drawing Blood, Allegories of
Modernism: Contemporary Drawing', *The Village Voice*,
New York, 3 March
Kaeppelin, Olivier, 'Richard Deacon', *Galeries*, Paris,
April/May

RICHARD DEACON
FOURSOME
31 JANUARY TO 14 MARCH 1992

PRIVATE VIEW
Thursday, 30 January 1992, from 6 to 8pm

LISSON GALLERY
67 Lisson St & 52-54 Bell St, London NW1
Telephone: 071 724 2739

Border 1991. Photo Volker Döhne

Minne, Michele, 'Villeneuve d'Ascq, Richard Deacon',
Art et Culture, France, June
Popelier, Bert, 'Een postmodernistische Brit', *De
Artsenkrant*, Germany, 23 June
'Richard Deacon in museum van Villeneuve d'Ascq', *De
Morgen*, Germany, 27 June
Foveau, Pascal, 'Le fabricateur', *Liberte-Dimanche*,
France, 28 June

Renton, Andrew, 'Richard Deacon, Overwrought Iron',
Flash Art, Milan, May/June
Dusinberre, Deke, 'Sticky Comparisons?', *Art Monthly*,
London, July/August

Heynen, Julian, 'Die schwierige Stadt und die
öffentliche kunst-momente eines Konfliktes', *Die
Stiftung der Sparhasse Krefeld*, Krefeld, Germany, May

Between Fiction and Fact, in progress, 1992

Archer, Michael, 'Documenta IX', *Art Monthly*, London,
July/August

Exhibitions and projects
1992-93

Cat. *Documenta IX*, (group) texts Jan Hoet, Denys Zacharopoulos, Pier Luigi Tazzi and Bart de Baere
Book, *Richard Deacon*, Centre National des Arts Plastiques and Editions du Regard, text by Lynne Cooke and Richard Deacon

Marian Goodman Gallery, New York (solo)

'Transform',
Kunstmuseum and **Kunsthalle Basel** (group)
Cat. *Bild Objekt Skulptur im 20 Jahrhundert*, text Julian Heynen

'One Step, Two Step',
Landspitze and **Nieuwmarkt**, Nordhorn
Commissioned by Stadt Nordhorn

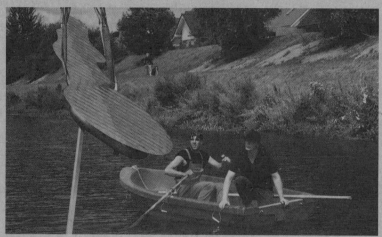

One Step, Two Step, in progress, 1992

1993
Galerie Arlogos, Nantes (solo)

'Zeitweise',
Mexicoplatz, Vienna
Commissioned by Stadt Wien

'New Sculptures/Nieuwe Beelden',
Middelheim Park, Antwerp. Commissioned by the City of Antwerp (group)
Cat. *New Sculptures/Nieuwe Beelden*, essay on Richard Deacon by Michael Tarantino

'Factory', dance collaboration with Hervé Robbe, set designed by Richard Deacon, costumes designed by Richard Deacon and Dominique Fabrègue; performed by La Companie le Marietta Secret at **La Ferme Du Boisson**, Paris, toured France
'Factory 93', video of production

'Only the Lonely and Other Shared Sculptures', (Bill Woodrow and Richard Deacon),
Chisenhale Gallery, London (tour to **Aspex Gallery**, Portsmouth) (group)
Cat. *Only the Lonely and Other Shared Sculptures*, texts Richard Deacon and Bill Woodrow

'Skulpturen 1987-1993',
Kunstverein Hannover, Orangerie, Herrenhauser Garten, Hannover (solo)

Selected articles and interviews
1992-93

Melrod, George, 'Richard Deacon at Marian Goodman', *Art in America*, New York, February, 1993

Berg, Stephen, 'Transform', *Kunstforum*, Germany, No 120

Richard Deacon', *Mizue*, Summer
Aoki, Hiroshi, 'Artmuseums' New Collection's - Tochigi Prefectural Museum of Fine Art', *Bijutsu Techno*, Tokyo, August
Francis, Richard, 'Richard Deacon and Engels; Three Footnotes', *Forum International*, Belgium, November/December
Potrc, Marjetica, 'From an Interview with Richard Deacon', *Kunst and Museum Journaal*, Amsterdam, Vol 4, No 3
'Richard Deacon', *Art Watching (Freestyle)*, Japan, Winter
Bruce D. Kurtz, *Contemporary Art 1965-1990*, Prentice Hall, New Jersey
Blazwick, Iwona, 'Living in a Material World (Madonna 'Material Girl' 1985)', *Kunst and Museum Journaal*, Amsterdam, Vol 4, No 3

1993

Messler, Norbert, 'New Sculptures', *Artforum*, New York, Vol XXXII, No 7
Bustard, James, 'Antwerp: The Cultural Tally after a Year', *The Art Newspaper*, London, January, 1994

Frétard, Dominique, 'Mariages dans L'Espace', *Le Monde*, Paris, 18 March
Louppe, Laurence, 'États de corps, états d'espaces', *Art Press*, Paris, No 179
Arvers, Fabienne, 'Factory à la Ferme', *Liberation*, France, 30 April

McEwan, John, 'From shadows to furrows lit by neon', *The Sunday Telegraph*, London, 30 May

Schwarz, Karin, 'Zum Sehen un Zum Tasten', *Nobilis*, Germany, October
'Wasser und Dschungel', *Stern*, Germany, No 42

Exhibitions and projects
1993-95

Cat. *Skulpturen/Sculptures 1987-1993*, various author

What Could Make Me Feel This Way A, in progress, 1993

'Richard Deacon and European Silver Tea and Coffeepots', **Feuerle**, Köln (solo)

'What Could Make Me Feel This Way'
The British School at Rome, Italy (solo)
Cat. *What Could Make Me Feel This Way*, text Pier Luigi Tazzi

'Kiss and Tell',
South Bank National Touring exhibition (solo)
Cat. *Kiss and Tell*, text Richard Cork

1994
Text, 'A propos de Toni Grand', in catalogue *Toni Grand*
Musée Jeu de Paume, Paris and **Camden Arts Centre**, London

'Only the Lonely and Other Shared Sculptures' (Bill Woodrow and Richard Deacon),
Sabine Wachters, Brussels (group)

'Till Brancusi',
Mälmo Konsthall, Sweden (group)
Cat. *Till Brancusi*, text Sune Nordgren

'Re Rebaudengo Sandretto Collection',
S. Antonio di Susa, Turin (group)

1995
'Atlas + This is Not a Story' (drawings and prints),
Customs House, South Shields (solo)

'Not Yet Beautiful',
L.A. Louver Gallery, Los Angeles (solo)

'ARS'95',
Museum of Contemporary Art, Helsinki (group)

'Drawing, Prints and Sculpture',
La Filature, Mulhouse (solo)

'Them and Us: Richard Deacon and Thomas Schütte',
Lisson Gallery, London (group)

'Decadence',
Konsthall Trondheim, Norway (group)

'12 British Sculptors',
Auditorio de Galicia, Santiago de Compostela, Spain (group)

Selected articles and interviews
1993-95

von Radziewsky, Elke, 'Stahlpfütze und Gedankenkörper', *Die Ziet*, Germany, No 43
'Unter die Haut', *Der Speigel*, Germany, 25 Oct, No 43
Böer, Claudia, 'Kunstverein Hannover: Verschlungene Skulpturen von Richard Deacon', *Kieler Nachrichten*, Germany, 21 October
Thiede, Veit-Mario, 'Für Sinne, Verstand und Gefühle', *Straubinger Tageblatt*, Germany, 25 October
Wintér, Peter, 'Auf der Achterbahn', *Donnerstag*, Germany, 28 October , No 251, Seite 37
Stoeber, Michael, 'Tausendfüßler und andere Monstrositäten', *Die Tageszeitung*, Germany, 16 November

1994

Lambrecht, Luk, 'Richard Deacon, Bill Woodrow: Sabine Wachters', *Flash Art*, Milan, Vol XXVII, No 176

1995

Knight, Christopher, 'Playful suggestive sculptures from one of today's finest', *Los Angeles Times*, 28 January

Richard Deacon and Bill Woodrow

Allthorpe-Guyton, Marjorie, *Richard Deacon*, Whitechapel Art Gallery, London, 1988

Anderson, Michael, 'Richard Deacon at the Museum of Contemporary Art', *Art Issues*, Los Angeles, April 1989

Angel Trenas, Miguel, 'Richard Deacon: Mis esculturas no esconden, permiten conocer su piel', *La Vanguardia*, Spain, 12 April, 1987

Aoki, Hiroshi, 'Artmuseums' New Collection's - Tochigi Prefectural Museum of Fine Art', *Bijutsu Techno*, Tokyo, August, 1992

Archer, Michael, 'Review, Whitechapel', *Art Monthly*, London, March, 1988

Archer, Michael, 'Harmony and Dislocation', *Art Monthly*, London, February, 1992

Archer, Michael, 'Documenta IX', *Art Monthly*, London, July/August, 1992

Auty, Giles, 'The Stamp of Official Approval', *The Spectator*, London, 5 December, 18 April, 1987

Baker, Kenneth, 'Physical Precision, notes on some recent sculpture', *Artspace*, September/October, 1990

Barker, Barry, *Falls the Shadow*, The Arts Council of Great Britain, London, 1986

Berg, Stephen, 'Transform', *Kunstforum*, Cologne, No 120, 1993

Bevan, Roger, 'Richard Deacon in London, Krefeld and Pittsburgh', *Modern Painters*, London, Spring, 1992

Bickers, Patricia, 'A Conversation with Richard Deacon', *Art Monthly*, London, No 83, 1985

Bickers, Patricia ' Interview with Richard Deacon about His Recent Public Sculpture', *Art Monthly*, London, October, 1991

Biggs, Lewis, *Objects and Sculpture*, ICA, London and Arnolfini Gallery, Bristol, 1981

Biggs, Lewis, 'Objects & Sculpture', *Arnolfini Review*, Bristol, June-July, 1981

Biggs, Lewis, *Transformations: New Sculpture from Britain*, The British Council, London,1983

Biggs, Lewis, *Entre el Objeto y la Imagen. Escultura Britanica Contemporanea*, The British Council and Ministerio de Cultura, Spain, 1986

Blacker, Kate, *The Sculpture Show*, Hayward and Serpentine Galleries, London, 1983

Blazwick, Iwona, *Objects and Sculpture*, ICA, London and Arnolfini Gallery, Bristol, 1981

Blazwick, Iwona, 'Living in a Material World (Madonna ` Material Girl' 1985)', *Kunst and Museum Journaal*, The Netherlands, Vol.4, No 3, 1992

Böer, Claudia, 'Kunstverein Hannover: Verschlungene Skulpturen von Richard Deacon', *Kieler Nachrichten*, 21 Oct, 1993

Brenson, Michael, 'Richard Deacon at Marian Goodman', *New York Times*, New York, 16 May, 1986

Brenson, Michael, 'Richard Deacon's Sculptures at the Marian Goodman Gallery', *New York Times*, 14 March, 1988

Brighton, Andrew, *Current Affairs: British Painting and Sculpture in the 1980s*, Museum of Modern Art, Oxford, 1987

Caldwell, John, *Richard Deacon*, The Carnegie Museum of Art, Pittsburgh, Pennsylvania, 1988

Cameron, Dan, 'Armleder, Martin, Deacon', *Flash Art*, Milan, No 130, 1986

Cohen, Françoise, *Brittanica. 30 ans de Sculpture*, Musée des Beaux Arts André Malraux, Le Havre, 1988

Collier, Caroline, 'Richard Deacon at the Riverside Studios', *Studio International*, vol 196, No 1004, 1984

Compton, Michael, *New Art*, Tate Gallery, London, 1983

Cooke, Lynne, 'Carolyne Kardia at Felicity Samuel, Richard Deacon at The Gallery, Brixton', *Artscribe*, London, No 24, 1980.

Cooke, Lynne, 'Reconsidering the New Sculpture', *Artscribe*, London, No 42, 1983

Cooke, Lynne, 'Richard Deacon: Lisson Gallery', *Art Monthly*, London, No 64, 1983

Cooke, Lynne, *Richard Deacon: Sculpture*, The Orchard Gallery, Derry, 1983

Cooke, Lynne, *Transformations: New Sculpture from Britain*, The British Council, London, 1983

Cooke, Lynne, 'Richard Deacon at the Riverside Studios', *Art in America*, New York, September, 1984

Cooke, Lynne, 'Impresa', *Flash Art*, No 130, 1986

Cooke, Lynne, 'What is Modern Sculpture?', *Artscribe*, London, No 60, 1986

Cooke, Lynne, *Brittanica. 30 ans de Sculpture*, Musée des Beaux Arts André Malraux, Le Havre, 1988

Cooke, Lynne, *Richard Deacon*, The Carnegie Museum of Art, Pittsburgh, Pennsylvania, 1988

Cooke, Lynne, *Richard Deacon*, Whitechapel Art Gallery, London, 1988

Cooke, Lynne, *Richard Deacon*, Centre National des Arts Plastiques and Editions du regard, 1992

Cooke, Lynne, *Starlit Waters*, Tate Gallery, Liverpool, 1988

Cork, Richard, 'Cragg, Woodrow and Deacon: Three Individuals', *Arts and Design*, No 11/12, 1987

Cork, Richard, *Kiss and Tell*, South Bank National Touring Exhibition, London, 1993

Cornall, John, 'Very Like a Whale: Meaning in Sculpture of Richard Deacon', *Alba*, No 6, Winter, 1987 Crichton, Fenella, *The Sculpture Show*, Hayward and Serpentine Galleries, London, 1983

De Loisy, Jean, *Art for Other People*, Musée d'art moderne de la Communité Urbaine de Lille, Villeneuve d'Ascq, 1992

De Monchaux, Paul, *The Sculpture Show*, Hayward and Serpentine Galleries, London, 1983

Deacon, Richard, in exhibition catalogue, *Jacqui Poncelet, New Ceramics*, Craft Council, 1981

Deacon, Richard, *Stuff Box Object, Richard Deacon 1972/73*, Chapter Arts Centre, Cardiff, 1984

Deacon, Richard, *For Those Who Have Eyes. Richard Deacon Sculptures 1980-86*, Aberystwyth Arts Centre, Wales, 1986

Deacon, Richard, *Skulptur Projekte in Munster*, texts also by other contributing artists, 1987

Deacon, Richard, *Britannia. Paintings and Sculptures from the 1980s*, The British Council, 1987

Deacon, Richard, *Richard Deacon*, The Carnegie Museum of Art, Pittsburgh, Pennsylvania, 1988

Deacon, Richard, Artist's Book: *Atlas: Gondwanaland and Eurasia*, Kunstnernes Hus, Oslo, 1990

Deacon, Richard, 'A Sculptor's View, Living in a Material World', essay in exhibition catalogue, *The Non-Objective World*, South Bank Centre, London, 1991

Deacon, Richard, *This Is Not a Story*, 'Platzverführung', Stadt Waiblingen, Hugo Mathaes, Verlag, Stuttgart, 1992

Deacon, Richard, *Richard Deacon*, Centre National des Arts Plastiques and Editions du regard, 1992

Deacon, Richard, *Only the Lonely and Other Shared Sculptures*, texts 1993

Deacon, Richard, *Skulpturen/ Sculptures 1987-1993*, Kunstverein Hannover, texts by various authors, 1993

Deacon, Richard, 'A propos de Toni Grand', in exhibition catalogue *Toni Grand*, Musée Jeu de Paume, Paris and Camden Arts Centre, London, 1994

Decter, Joshua, *Juxtapositions: Recent Sculpture from England and Germany*, PSI, The Institute for Art and Urban Resources Inc, New York, 1987

Dexter, Emma, 'United Kingdom, Richard Deacon, Lisson Gallery', *Sculpture*, May-June, 1992

Dimitrijevic, Nena, 'Sculpture after Evolution', *Flash Art*, Milan, April-May, 1984

Dimitrijevic, Nena, *The Sculpture Show*, Hayward and Serpentine Galleries, London, 1983

Donnely, Micky, 'Richard Deacon Sculpture', Orchard Gallery, *Circa*, Dublin, No 11, 1983

Durand, Regis, 'Richard Deacon: le grand "fabricateur"', *Art Press*, Paris, 134, 1988

Enrici, Michel, 'Richard Deacon: Un Pan de Labeur, Inestimable', *Galeries Magazine*, Paris, No 30, 1989

Enrici, Michel, *Richard Deacon*, Galerie Arlogos, Nantes, France, 1986

Eustace, Katherine, *Let's Not Be Stupid*, Mead Gallery, University of Warwick, 1991

Faure-Walker, Caryn, 'Interview with Richard Deacon', *Aspects*, No 17, 1982

Feaver, William, 'Richard Deacon, Whitechapel Art Gallery', *ARTnews*, New York, April, 1988

Ferbos, Catherine, 'Sculptures in Between - le paysage', *Artstudio*, Paris, Autumn, 1988

Fonce, Jan, 'For Those Who Have Eyes', *Artefactum*, Belgium, September/October, 1988

Foster, Tony, *New Works for Different Places: Four Cities Project*, TSWA - Four Cities Project, London, 1990

Francis, Mark, 'Objects & Sculpture', *Art Monthly*, London, No 48, 1981

Francis, Mark, *Transformations: New Sculpture from Britain*, The British Council, London, 1983

Francis, Richard (interview), *Richard Deacon, Talking About Those Who Have Ears No 2 and Other Works*, Patrons of New Art, Tate Gallery, London, 1985

Francis, Richard, *The Poetic Object: Richard Deacon, Shirazeh Houshiary and Anish Kapoor*, The Douglas Hyde Gallery, Dublin, 1985

Francis, Richard, *Britannia. Paintings and Sculptures from the 1980s*, The British Council, 1987

Francis, Richard, 'Richard Deacon and Engels; Three Footnotes', *Forum International*, Belgium, November-December, 1992

Furse, John, 'Richard Deacon', *Art Monthly*, London, No 132, 1990

Grenier, Catherine, *Brittanica. 30 ans de Sculpture*, Musée des Beaux Arts André Malraux, Le Havre, 1988

Hall, James, 'Organs of Desire', *The Independent*, London, 18 February 1992

Harrison, Charles, 'Sculpture, Design and Three-Dimensional Work', *Artscribe*, London, No 58, 1986

Harrison, Charles, *Arts Magazine*, New York, No 109, March, 1988

Harrison, Charles, *Richard Deacon. Recent Sculpture 1985-1988*, Bonnefanten Museum, Maastricht, 1987

Harvey, Jonathan, *New Works for Different Places: Four Cities Project*, TSWA - Four Cities Project, London/Plymouth, 1990

Hatton, Brian, 'Richard Deacon, Whitechapel London', *Flash Art*, Milan, May/June, 1988

Headly, Gill, *British Art Now: A Subjective View*, The British Council, 1990

Heiss, Alanna, *Juxtapositions: Recent Sculpture from England and Germany*, PSI, The Institute for Art and Urban Resources Inc, New York, 1987

Heynen, Julian, 'Die schwierige Stadt und die öffentliche kunstmomente eines Konfliktes', *Die Stiftung der Sparhasse Krefeld*, Krefeld, May, 1992

Heynen, Julian, *Bild Objekt Skulptur im 20 Jahrhundert*, Kunstmuseum and Kunsthalle Basel, 1992

Heynen, Julian, *Richard Deacon, Museum Haus Lange und Haus Esters, Krefeld*, interview, 1991

Heynen, Julian, *Skulpturen fur Krefeld I*, Museum Haus Esters, Krefeld, 1989

Heynen, Julian, *Weitersehen*, Museum Haus Esters and Museum Haus Lange, Krefeld, 1990

Hutchinson, John, *Inheritance and Transformation*, New Musuem of Contemporary Art for Ireland, Dublin, 1991

Jacob, Mary Jane, *A Quiet Revolution: British Sculpture Since 1965*, Museum of Contemporary Art, Chicago and San Francisco Museum of Modern Art, 1987

Jocks, Heinz-Norbert, 'Weitersehen', *Kunstforum*, Cologne, Bd.111, January/February, 1990